DOING
JUSTICE

DOING JUSTICE

Congregations and Community Organizing

Dennis A. Jacobsen

*"He has told you, O mortal, what
is good;
and what does the Lord require
of you
but to do justice, and to love
kindness,
and to walk humbly with your
God?"*

— Micah 6:8

FORTRESS PRESS
Minneapolis

Cover art: "Crowd #16" by Diana Ong, copyright © 2001 by SuperStock, Inc. Used by permission.
Cover and interior design: Beth Wright

Scripture quotations are from the New Revised Standard Version Bible, copyright © 1989 by the Division of Christian Education of the National Council of the Churches of Christ in the USA, and are used by permission.

Library of Congress Cataloging-in-Publication Data

Jacobsen, Dennis, date—
   Doing justice : congregations and community organizing / Dennis Jacobsen.
     p. cm.
   Includes bibliographical references and index.
   ISBN 0-8006-3244-3 (alk. paper)
    1. Sociology, Christian. I. Title.
  BV 625 .J33 2001
  261.8—dc21

                         2001023888

The paper used in this publication meets the minimum requirements of American National Standard for Information Sciences — Permanence of Paper for Printed Library Materials, ANSI Z329.48-1984.

Manufactured in the U.S.A.   AF1-3244
05   04   03   02   3   4   5   6   7   8   9   10

For Lynn, Nora, and Laureena:
Your love sustains me
when I am weary
of trying
to do justice.

CONTENTS

"I will stand at my watchpost, and station myself on the rampart; I will keep watch to see what he will say to me, and what he will answer concerning my complaint. Then the Lord answered me and said: Write the vision; make it plain on tablets, so that a runner may read it." (Hab. 2:1-2)

This book was written on the run, here and there between pastoral responsibilities, devotion to spouse and children, and various efforts for justice in the public arena. It is intended as an introductory theology of congregation-based community organizing for those who are similarly on the run. Any vision found on these pages flows from the hundreds of clergy, laity, and organizers whom I have come to know and admire in the faith-based struggle for a just society in this country.

Since 1992 I have been honored to be one of the presenters at each annual Gamaliel National Clergy Training in Techny, Illinois. In this setting, my colleagues and I in the Gamaliel network of congregation-based community organizations have reflected on some of the basic concepts of community organizing from a theological and biblical perspective. Several chapters in this book flow from presentations that I have offered at Techny. Those familiar with organizing training events will recognize the standard concepts that are considered in this book: the world as it is, the world as it should be, the public arena, power, self-interest, one-on-ones, agitation. Other chapters consider additional concepts key to the organizing enterprise.

I owe a debt of gratitude to so many people who have influenced my biblical understanding of justice ministry that it would take another book to name them all. I would be particularly remiss if I did not name a few. Thanks to Daniel Berrigan who taught me, among other things, that the claim to be a Christian carries with it the cost of where conscience leads. Thanks to Gregory Galluzzo who entrusts me with the role of director of the Gamaliel National Clergy Caucus and who sees in me more than I see in myself. Thanks to Dick Snyder and other faculty of New York Theological Seminary for training me to think theologically about congregation-based community organizing in my doctor of ministry studies. Thanks to the good people of MICAH and of Incarnation Lutheran Church in Milwaukee with whom I have struggled for justice and experienced a gracious sense of community. Thanks to Rick Deines and my colleagues in the Milwaukee Lutheran Coalition who have helped me to integrate justice and congregational ministry.

Thanks to all who have been merciful to me when my passion for justice has made me heavy-handed with them.

CHAPTER 1

The World as It Is

"Jesus said to them, 'My time has not yet come, but your time is always here. The world cannot hate you, but it hates me because I testify against it that its works are evil.'" (John 7:6-7)

"After this I saw another angel coming down from heaven, having great authority; and the earth was made bright with his splendor. He called out with a mighty voice, 'Fallen, fallen is Babylon the great! . . . For all the nations have drunk of the wine of the wrath of her fornication, and the kings of the earth have committed fornication with her, and the merchants of the earth have grown rich from the power of her luxury.' Then I heard another voice from heaven saying, 'Come out of her, my people, so that you do not take part in her sins.'" (Rev. 18:1-4)

The world, as it is, is the enemy of God. The world, as it is, is the enemy of the people of God. The world, as it is, is the enemy of those who, while claiming no belief in God, are devoted to creating a just society and act with such courageous conscience that they put the institutional church to shame. A great tension exists between the world as it is and those believers and nonbelievers who are "in the world but not of the world." It is so because the world, as it is, is driven by abusive power, consuming greed, relentless violence, and narcissistic pride. The world as it is employs nationalism, propaganda, racism, civil religion, and class enmity to bolster entrenched systems, corporations, and institutions. All of which are offensive to God and to those who seek to do what is just.

Throughout the centuries those who have faithfully witnessed to Jesus have learned all too well why the Greek word used for "witness" in the New Testament transliterates as "martyr." But certainly it is not only obedient Christians who have found that the world is their enemy. People of conscience in every society have suffered the affliction of being enemies of the State, held suspect, imprisoned, brutalized, exiled, executed. The Buddhist monk and peace activist Thich Nhat Hanh speaks a word that all people of conscience understand: "We are the loving adversaries of every regime."

Most Christians in the United States are lulled into imagining that here it is different. In this nation, do we not see the defender of religious freedom, of freedom of speech, of democracy? In this nation, do we not see the hope of the world, the defender of truth, the strongest society in history? In this nation, do we not see a friend of God? Surely here Christians may make peace with the world.

Perhaps those who feel at home in the United States are victims of the despotic democracy predicted by the French political scientist, Alexis de Tocqueville, in 1831. He foresaw:

> an innumerable multitude of men, all equal and alike, incessantly endeavoring to procure the petty and paltry pleasures with which they glut their lives. Each of them, living apart, is as a stranger to the fate of all the rest; his children and his private friends constitute to him the whole of mankind. As for the rest of his fellow citizens, he is close to them, but he does not see them; he touches them, but he does not feel them; he exists only in himself and for himself alone. . . .[1]

Those Christians who feel at home in the United States can do so only because they have buffered themselves from the brutal conditions of poverty, blinded themselves to the realities of racism, and deluded themselves into imagining that the vast military force of this country is the agent of justice. Many such Christians worship the idol of prosperity and have quieted their conscience in return for lives of relative ease and material comfort.

I had a nightmare recently in which I dreamed I was living in a house that was not my house. In the kitchen of this house, I sat in conversation with my wife and a friend who directs the Lutheran Coalition of ministries in Milwaukee. My friend asked me if I weep like one of the other urban pastors weeps. I said, "No. I no longer cry." He became very agitated at my response. I went down into the basement to call an insurance adjuster about a man that had been recently murdered by a fourteen-year-old boy. While on the phone, I heard the squeal of tires. Looking out the basement window, I saw that two cars had turned to block off the street in front of the house. Between the cars was a member of my congregation who had been a Vice Lord. Gang bangers got out of the cars, weapons drawn, and started to chase him into the house. Fearing that my wife would be caught in a cross fire, I screamed out a warning.

When I awoke in the middle of the night, I tried to sort out this dream. On one level it seemed a signal that I was shutting down emotionally to the horrors around me in my daily ministry. It also obviously touched on my fears and insecurity. Perhaps the nightmare is also something about my resistance to facing the world as it is. To live in a house that is not my house is my attempt to live where I do not belong. It is my attempt to create an individualized, safe, secure life for myself and my family removed from the violence that afflicts the urban poor. To no longer be able to cry about the daily horrors I encounter is a sign of spiritual death. It is a psychic numbing, an emotional distancing, an unconscionable removal from the lives of those who suffer. It is the encroachment of America on my soul.

In the middle of a First Communion Class, a ten-year-old boy from the neighborhood said to me: "Hell is living in the ghetto with all its violence. Heaven is living in a safe neighborhood." Even though such a statement disregards both the heavenly qualities of many who live in the ghetto and the hellish aspects of life for many who live in safe neighborhoods, it nonetheless offers a clear truth. In this country, a line divides those who are trapped in urban ghettoes from those who have the economic luxury to live in relative ease. And the perception of life in the United States has a great deal to do with which side of the dividing line one lives.

How does one describe life on the ghettoized end of the dividing line? I think of the nine-year-old boy I visited, whose family was living on the third floor of an abandoned apartment building in a room without plumbing, heat, or electricity. His arm was broken and in a cast but he would still go into the basement each morning, fill a bucket with water from a leaking pipe, and carry it up three flights of stairs to his family.

I think of Billy who is single and usually unemployed or working menial, temporary jobs. His income is too little and unpredictable to rent his own apartment so he stays with some acquaintances who smoke crack cocaine whenever they can. One day when I dropped him off at his place, he got out of the car carrying a bag of emergency food, motioned toward his apartment and said, "Welcome to my little corner of hell."

I think of Teresa whose only income is a meager disability check she gets for her eight-year-old boy. His emotional outbursts are frequent, unpredictable, and so severe that she is summoned to his school at least three times a week and thus can't hold down even a part-time job. Unable to afford her own apartment, she doubled up with a family and then had to fend off unwelcome advances from the man of the house. One day, having no money for diapers and hearing that the downtown WIC office was offering them for free, she walked thirty blocks with her two-year-old and three-year-old daughters, only to be turned away empty-handed.

I think of visiting Gary in the county jail, where he was awaiting trial on felony charges. Not having seen him in months, I was taken aback by how haggard he looked and by how much weight he had lost. Weeping, he spoke of being homeless and addicted. Too afraid of being preyed upon if he fell asleep, he would wander the streets at night, high on cocaine. In jail he was doing what he could to avoid the gang bangers. He was finding some solace in one prisoner who, while dying of AIDS, was willing to listen to Gary and offer emotional support. "It's hard in here," Gary said. "But it's better than being on the streets."

I think of a recent visit to Deborah. We sat in her living room. I asked how things were going. "Not well," she said. Her daughter, who is a prostitute and drug addict, was pregnant once again. (I have already baptized five cocaine babies birthed by her daughter.) The city building inspector had cited her house for thirty code violations and was threatening to begin fines. She was without any money to make repairs. (I had cautioned Deborah against buying this house. Her income was so limited and her credit so poor that the only home loan she could obtain was from a loan shark mortgage company at 16 percent interest. Her monthly payments were so high that she had no money for the required repairs.) Deborah told me that two days prior to my visit she had observed her forty-fourth birthday. That day she went with her teenage son to see his parole officer. She watched as her son was suddenly handcuffed and taken into custody for parole violation. Out on parole for a few months after serving two years, he had been gang banging again and not attending high school.

Seeing her son taken away was so upsetting to Deborah that she suffered a mild stroke and was taken to the hospital. (She has been suffering for years from diabetes and dangerously high blood pressure.) She has an ongoing concern that the grandchildren she is raising will be taken away by social workers and placed in separate foster homes. Raising these children, with all the complications particular to cocaine babies, is more taxing than one can possibly imagine. Deborah's health is broken. She has not had a vacation in ten years. She lacks sufficient income to pay her bills. Her family is in disarray. Her only lifeline is her faith in Jesus and the concern of the church.

For Christians who do not live in poverty, the challenge is to view the world as it is from the underside, from the bottom, from the vantage point of the poor. Otherwise, at home in their society, they face the accusation of Jesus: "The world cannot hate you, but it hates me. . . ." How indeed can the world hate the Christian who is at peace with the world? In fact, the world values such a Christian. He or she is useful to the status quo. Such a Christian, attentive to the propaganda of the State, has closed his or her ears to the voice from heaven regarding Babylon: "Come out of her, my people, so that you do not take part in her sins" (Rev. 18:4).

How does one come out of Babylon? In the first instance, this command suggests a perpetual state of internal exile. The status of the faithful Christian is always one of being an alien in a strange land, always feeling unease with the disease of the culture. To come out of Babylon is to live in a constant state of resistance to classism, racism, and militarism. To come out of Babylon is to connect with a community of faith and faithfulness. To come out of Babylon is to act in accordance with one's conscience.

The world as it is will not be essentially changed until the *eschaton*, the end times. The fall of Babylon announced by the angel in Revelation 18 is an eschatological pronouncement. To come out of Babylon is not to make Babylon fall. The power to make Babylon finally fall is beyond human capacity. Whenever an empire falls within history, Babylon emerges resilient within the new regime. Such is the tenacity of Babylon in its hold on the world. As Daniel Berrigan points out: "To biblical faith there remain only small gestures of mitigation, of resistance, of unmasking, of holding accountable."[2] For the person who resists Babylon, the danger is that the good that can be done is too modest to be esteemed. The temptation is always a devotion to the consequential and the useful, the sweeping change and the grand scale action. Despite all best efforts, Babylon endures. The world as it is remains the enemy of God.

The world as it is operates out of domineering power, crass self-interest, and quid pro quo. Mayors, corporate executives, and union leaders may indeed be people of faith who in their personal relationships and private lives seek to live according to the ethical teachings of Jesus. Personally they may be quite charitable, forgiving, and exemplary in their love. But in their public life they are constrained to adopt a different ethic. Decisions are made with a different criteria dominant. What will expand my power and the power of my government? What serves my self-interest and the self-interest of my corporation? What is the quid pro quo at work in cutting this or that deal?

The world as it is has no interest in heeding the prophetic warnings of the faithful community. Moral suasion alone does not move government or corporate America. If moral suasion is backed by a substantial number of voters or shareholders and captures the attention of the media, then power and self-interest are engaged. But apart from such dynamics of public pressure, moral suasion represents little more than an annoyance to the powers that be. The world as it is ignores the prophets of God or disposes of them as it sees fit.

The world as it is co-opts religion for its own purposes. Before President Bush announced his decision to declare war on Iraq, Billy Graham was invited to stay overnight at the White House. Are we to believe that the President was engaged in a soul-searching night of discerning prayer? At work here was the classic use of the court prophet, *Gott mit uns*, the public appearance of moral authority and divine blessing. In essence, it was no different from Islamic clerics offering their assent to Saddam Hussein's claim that this action was a *jihad*, a holy war.

When the Monica Lewinsky affair became public, the Rev. Jesse Jackson was summoned to the White House as pastoral counselor for the Clintons. All well and good. But the political orchestration seemed transparent when Reverend Jackson then addressed the media concerning the performance of his pastoral duties. No Nathan the Prophet here, boldly confronting the sexual misconduct of the nation's ruler (2 Sam. 12:1-15).

I declined an invitation by my well-intentioned Congressman to be his guest at the National Prayer Breakfast in Washington, D.C. He is an effective, decent legislator. But what is the point of gathering clergy from around the country to dine and pray with Congress? Even though Congress serves the interests of the rich and of corporate America and wars on the poor at home and abroad, do not clergy offer tacit approval and moral blessing when they attend the National Prayer Breakfast?

When I served as a parish pastor in Jersey City, New Jersey, I learned that forty-five of the inner-city clergy were on the city payroll. When the mayoral election drew near, his Honor called in the chips. The bought-off clergy dutifully gathered for a group photo shoot at City Hall. These photographs were circulated throughout the inner city. Low-income voters, seeing their photogenic pastors standing beside the beaming mayor, were either ashamed of their pastors or seduced into voting for a man whose official decisions were worsening their conditions.

The world as it is, the enemy of God and under the judgment of God, is ironically loved by God. God seeks the salvation of the world. The mystery of forgiveness is at work in Revelation 21:24 where the seer envisions the kings of the earth bringing the glory of the nations into the heavenly Jerusalem. This promise follows the blood bath of Armageddon (Rev. 19:11-21) where the kings of the earth are slain in battle by the rider on a white horse whose name is "The Word of God." We are surprised, then, to see these defiant, slain kings reappearing in Revelation 21, bringing their glory into the holy city. The kings are not only forgiven, their glory is received and honored. All that has defied God in history is redeemed.

The world as it is has a glory to it that is worthy of being in heaven and worthy of the incarnate presence of God on earth. Human achievements in art, science, architecture, law, government, religion, music, and education are indeed glorious. Purged of *hubris*, oppression, and defiance, human culture, part and parcel of the world as it is, adorns the holy city. The world, as it is, is loved by God and eschatologically redeemed.

CHAPTER 2

The World as It Should Be

"Then he began to speak, and taught them, saying: 'Blessed are the poor in spirit, for theirs is the kingdom of heaven. Blessed are those who mourn, for they will be comforted. Blessed are the meek, for they will inherit the earth. Blessed are those who hunger and thirst for righteousness, for they will be filled. Blessed are the merciful, for they will receive mercy. Blessed are the pure in heart, for they will see God. Blessed are the peacemakers, for they will be called the children of God. Blessed are those who are persecuted for righteousness' sake, for theirs is the kingdom of heaven.'" (Matt. 5:2-10)

"Pilate asked him, 'So you are a king?' Jesus answered, 'You say that I am a king. For this I was born, and for this I came into the world, to testify to the truth. Everyone who belongs to the truth listens to my voice.' Pilate asked him, 'What is truth?'" (John 18:37-38)

The world as it should be is in direct opposition to the world as it is. The world as it should be is rooted in truth, love, and community. In the world as it should be, the voice of conscience is heard. In the world as it should be, people act according to the values of their faith. In the world as it should be, fairness and mutuality reign. The world as it should be is God's dream engaging the nightmare that the world has become.

Our English word *person* comes from the Greek word *persona*. The persona was the mask held before the face of the actor in Greek theater. In the world as it should be, the persona is removed. People are able to trust each other sufficiently to be transparent and exposed. People are not forced into the psychic splitting that occurs in the world as it is. People can live truthfully, honestly, and with integrity as authentic persons.

People long for such a world and suffer because they do not find it. Lawyers, much maligned, are caught between the world as it should be and the world as it is. A recent study found that 11 percent of lawyers consider suicide at least once a month. Lawyers are more subject to depression than any other profession. Lawyers drink too much. Why? In part, this response is due to the psychic conflict caused by entering the legal profession with a devotion to the high ideals of justice and the law only to sink into a legal morass of deceit, dishonesty, corruption, ambition, and billable hours.

When I was a young minister, I had a passion for the world as it should be. As a campus pastor at SUNY at Plattsburgh, I became involved in the defense committee for Martin Sostre, a political prisoner at Clinton Correctional Facility, a New York maximum security prison in nearby Dannemora (named "Little Siberia" by the inmates). An activist in the African American community, Sostre had been framed by the Buffalo police on drug charges in the aftermath of the 1968 riots. He was sentenced to twenty to forty years. I became involved when Sostre was put on trial in Plattsburgh with charges of felony assault against seven prison guards.

For the past five years Sostre had been imprisoned in H Block, the punitive segregation unit of Clinton Correctional Facility, for wearing a quarter-inch goatee and refusing to submit to a rectal search. Summoned to testify in federal court in Manhattan on behalf of another prisoner who had been beaten, Sostre was required to have a rectal search upon his return to H Block. He refused. Seven guards forced the search on him. When Sostre charged them with assault, the guards predictably claimed that Sostre had in fact assaulted them.

Convinced of Sostre's innocence, I became involved in his defense committee. This involvement drew some media attention. I was contacted by the two Catholic chaplains at Clinton Correctional Facility and invited to their home in Dannemora for dinner. During the meal I became animated when the discussion turned to Sostre. One of the chaplains, Fr. Cormac Walsh, paused with fork in hand, looked at me with a sudden realization in his eyes, and said, "You actually believe that he is innocent, don't you?" I learned that Father Walsh had been the most highly decorated military chaplain in the Korean War. Years as a prison chaplain in the sordid environment of Dannemora had worn him down. He was obsequious to the guards and the warden. He drank too much.

For some reason our interaction breathed fire into the dying embers within him. A week later Father Walsh contacted me to indicate that he would testify on Sostre's behalf at his trial. He had heard things in H Block that attested to Sostre's innocence. The day after his testimony, Father Walsh went to work at the prison only to find that his office had been ransacked by guards looking for "contraband." He was summoned by the warden and told that due to security reasons he would no longer be allowed to visit in H Block without being accompanied by a guard.

Isolated in the prison, Father Walsh was also treated as a pariah in Dannemora. To my shame, I made no effort to reach out to him. He died of a heart attack a few months later. Sostre was found guilty and sentenced to an additional seven years in prison. My perception of the world as it should be encountered the world as it is.

For about a year, I drove to Dannemora each Sunday afternoon with a group of college students for a Bible study with prisoners at the annex of Clinton Correctional Facility. One day I received a letter from one of the prisoners describing in disturbing detail a retaliatory action by guards against inmates who had chosen to wear black armbands on the anniversary of the Attica uprising. The guards high-handcuffed several prisoners and beat them. Other prisoners were forced to walk a gauntlet between a line of guards who beat them with clubs. One prisoner was handcuffed and then thrown down a flight of stairs. His leg was broken in the fall.

Because I knew several of these prisoners, I felt as though I had to take some action. The wife of the deputy warden was active in the Newman Center where I served as campus pastor to the Protestant students. Pilar was a wonderful woman. I thought perhaps I could approach her husband as a Christian and get a Christian response. I made an appointment with him. When I entered his office, he seemed nervous. I showed him the letter, expressed my distress at the actions of the guards as reported by the prisoner that I knew from my Bible study group, and told him that I was hoping that he would respond as a Christian to this situation. He put the letter, unread, into his desk drawer, thanked me for coming, and showed me the door. A few days later Pilar told me that the warden was angry at her husband for meeting with me. I never heard of any investigation into the actions of the guards. A week later I received a letter from the warden informing me that I could no longer conduct my Bible study at Clinton Correctional Facility.

The world as it should be may have moral force, but it usually lacks power to effect change in the world as it is. Seeing the world as it should be rarely transforms the way the real world looks.

Those who operate only on the plane of conscience and truth may be faithful in their vision but they will have a limited impact on an impure world. While it is true that "without a vision the people perish," those devoted to the world as it should be need great moral strength to endure the ongoing rejection of their vision.

As I write these words, Philip Berrigan, now seventy-four years old, is back in prison on a two-year sentence for entering the Bath Iron Works with five other peace activists, climbing aboard an Aegis destroyer, and using hammers to symbolically beat the weapons system into plowshares. The Aegis destroyer is a surface ship with a nuclear arsenal capable of vaporizing a continent. Who would deny the moral truth of these peace activists' vision? Which sane person does not see the imperative of a world free of nuclear weapons? And yet Philip Berrigan and his comrades are in prison while the Pentagon goes about its death-serving business as usual. The world as it is would rather perish than embrace a moral vision.

The church has a responsibility to point the world as it is to the world as it should be. Heroes and heroines of the faith, such as Martin Luther King, Jr., Oscar Romero, the Berrigans, and Dorothy Day, offer a clarity of vision and moral force that is desperately needed by the jaded world as it is. Without seers of the world as it should be, only the cynicism of *real politick* remains. Despite the ongoing rejection of its moral vision, the church must continue to see the world through the eyes of faith. If the church is seduced by the world as it is into abandoning its vision of the world as it should be, then it has abandoned its calling, its mission, and its Lord.

My daughter, Nora, once had a dream of heaven. In her dream was a garden-like field with lovely trees. Under each tree children were playing. Jesus was under one of the trees laughing and playing with some children. Hearing this description, I asked if she saw any adults in the heaven of her dream. "No adults," Nora answered firmly. I asked her, "Why not?" "Well, Dad, doesn't it say that you have to turn and become children in order to enter the kingdom of heaven? Besides, why would Jesus want to spend eternity with a bunch of boring adults?"

In a world where 40,000 children die of hunger-related causes every day, the world as it should be has an abiding concern for children and for their right to have a playful present and a human future. A Native American tradition says that we must act in a way that gives thought to the impact of our actions on the next seven generations. Such solidarity with children and with children yet unborn is the only way to offer them a future worth entering.

The world as it should be is childlike in its innocence. This state of innocence is not to be confused with pseudo-innocence, a particular affliction of many Christians. Pseudo-innocence lacks the courage to see the world as it is. Pseudo-innocence imagines that the world is essentially good, that war is waged for moral purpose, that the poor cause their poverty, that race relations will be transformed through friendliness.

Pseudo-innocence is undaunted in its cheery approach to relationships, and bewildered and useless when it comes to systemic injustice.

Martin Luther King, Jr., with reference to Paul Tillich, observed that although power without love is tyranny, love without power is sentimentality. Sentimentality is the face of pseudo-innocence. Jesus said that we must be "as wise as serpents and as innocent as doves." Those who have a faithful vision of the world as it should be see the world as it is for what it is. They have the wisdom of serpents, but they retain a childlike innocence in their actions. They are willing to engage power in the service of love. And power joined to love can create justice.

This power merged with love was the strategic brilliance of the nonviolent campaign of Dr. King and of the thousands of people who carried that campaign toward its goal of civil rights. The childlike innocence of the world as it should be withstood the brutal realities of racist crowds, police dogs, beatings, and jail. Power tactics of direct action, boycotts, marches, media attention, judicial appeals, and shrewd negotiation were combined with nonviolent love to create historic advances in justice in the arena of civil rights.

Sometimes the world as it should be can have limited, positive impact on the world as it is. It is likely to happen only when love enjoins power in the interests of justice, and this assumes a willingness to engage the rough and tumble public arena of the world as it is.

CHAPTER 3

Engaging the Public Arena

"Go therefore and make disciples of all nations, baptizing them in the name of the Father and of the Son and of the Holy Spirit, and teaching them to obey everything that I have commanded you." (Matt. 28:19-20)

"The Spirit of the Lord is upon me, because he has anointed me to bring good news to the poor. He has sent me to proclaim release to the captives and recovery of sight to the blind, to let the oppressed go free, to proclaim the year of the Lord's favor." (Luke 4:18-19)

As a parish pastor, I love the sanctuary. It holds a calming, quiet beauty. One may hear shooting in the streets but in the sanctuary people share the peace. Outside is abusive, vulgar language. Inside language is sacred. Outside is gross inequality. Inside everyone stands equal in confession and kneels equal at the altar. Outside is a maddening, chaotic pace. Inside is orderly, liturgical time. Outside are the words of politicians. Inside is the word of God. I resonate to the words of Psalm 84: "How lovely is your dwelling place, O Lord of hosts! My soul longs, indeed it faints for the courts of the Lord . . . For a day in your courts is better than a thousand elsewhere."

Children of poverty are drawn to the sanctuary. They come, often without their parents or guardians. They come, with little encouragement or invitation. They come, often out of destructive, abusive households. They come because in the sanctuary they experience beauty, peacefulness, warmth, affirmation: the presence of God.

I am struck by the impact of the sanctuary on those who enter it. I have seen drunks, addicts, and criminals become subdued and attentive when they enter the sanctuary. Some fear it, as if they will be stricken by God for entering unworthy into a holy place. When congregants approach the altar for communion, I am moved to tears at times by the aggregate pain of the private lives made known to me as pastor. And I am struck by the hope, the determination, the trust in God that these congregants find in the sanctuary. How lovely is your dwelling place, O Lord of hosts.

But the attraction of the sanctuary can become a seduction. The sanctuary can be exploited and used to create false catharsis instead of authentic hope. The liturgy can be a vehicle for entering a disembodied drama instead of an incarnational vision. The sanctuary may serve only as a comfortable substitute for the harsh realities outside its walls. A mystery religion may be the result, void of any power to impact the world as it is.

Biblically speaking, the preeminent activity of the church is in the public arena, *not* in the sanctuary. The Holy Spirit calls and gathers the church and sends the church into the world with the liberating gospel of Jesus Christ. The Holy Spirit takes the church into the public arena so that the church can be the church. The explosive outpouring of the Holy Spirit at Pentecost and the subsequent narrative of the book of Acts are powerful descriptions of the emerging church engaging the public arena, witnessing to the resurrected Lord Jesus amidst principalities and powers, and paying dearly for its witness through persecution and imprisonment. To resist this summons to public life is to resist the Holy Spirit.

The church enters the public arena because it is mandated to do so by the Great Commission of Jesus. The church is sent by its Lord to "make disciples of all nations, baptizing . . . and teaching them to observe all that I have commanded you." This commission has nothing to do with church growth. The primary concern of the church in the public arena is not to find more members to fill the pews of the sanctuary. The church is sent into the public arena with the ethical imperatives of Jesus. The church is to proclaim the kingdom of God over against the kingdoms of the world. The church is to make disciples who actually live by and observe the teachings of its Lord.

The evangelistic mission of the church conforms to Jesus' own mission. The Spirit of the Lord who anointed Jesus "to bring good news to the poor . . . to proclaim release to the captives and recovery of sight to the blind, to let the oppressed go free" sends the church into the public arena with the same mission as its Lord. The evangelistic proclamation of the church must be liberative, must offer good news to the poor, must be faithful to the ethics of Jesus. Evangelistic efforts that claim to flow from the Great Commission but ignore or violate the Sermon on the Mount are not only ignoble but also heretical.

Dietrich Bonhoeffer wrote from his prison cell: "Our church has been fighting in these years only for its self-preservation, as though that were an end in itself. [Now it is] incapable of taking the word of reconciliation and redemption to humankind and the world." Although the horrors of

the Holocaust cannot honestly be compared to the suffering of those living in poverty in this country, the church by and large in our society is no
different from the church in Nazi Germany. The accommodation and
silence of the church amidst Nazi atrocities are paralleled by the accommodation and silence of the church in this country amidst a calculated
war against the poor.

Self-preservation and church growth are as much the central concern
of the church in this society as they were in Nazi Germany. And that central concern often obscures or defines the church's activity in the public
arena. But what does it signify for the church to be concerned only about
its growth and prosperity amidst growing poverty and escalating violence?
How can the church be concerned only with its own growth and not publicly engage and confront those forces that oppress the people of God? As
Bonhoeffer wrote, "the church is the church only when it exists for others." Self-preservation is antithetical to the cross of Jesus Christ.

The church focused only on self-preservation may indeed grow and
prosper but it will do so at the cost of betraying its Lord and belying its
identity. It may save its institutional life while losing its soul. It risks no
longer being the church, becoming instead a pseudo-church, a corporate
business that markets a product. In a revealing statement to a reporter,
the senior pastor of a mega-church in suburban Phoenix was quoted as
calling his congregants his "clientele."

The church enters the public arena in order to be the church, in order
to be true to itself, in order to be faithful to its Lord, in order to heed the
summons of the Holy Spirit. When the church faithfully enters the public arena, it enters what Bonhoeffer calls a "this-worldliness . . . living
unreservedly in life's duties, problems, successes and failures, experiences and perplexities. In so doing, we throw ourselves completely into
the arms of God, taking seriously not our own sufferings but those of God
in the world." The church enters the "this-worldliness" of the public
arena because God is encountered in the encounter with those who suffer in the world. Jesus was born not in a church but in a stable. Jesus died,
not of a heart attack from too many high cholesterol church dinners, but
of crucifixion as an enemy of the Roman empire. The public arena is
God's arena.

Who takes the local church into the public arena if not the pastor? If
the pastoral leadership of the local church is resistant to a public arena
ministry, even the best-intentioned laity will be blocked or deflated in
their efforts to engage their congregation in public arena issues. The

ambivalence, reluctance, or disdain of most clergy toward the public arena keeps most churches in the sanctuary.

Why are most clergy unwilling to lead their churches into the public arena? Perhaps we can draw some insight from the mythical theologian Franz Bibfeldt.[1] Bibfeldt was invented as a fake footnote to a term paper at my alma mater, Concordia Theological Seminary in St. Louis, in 1947. Occasional references to him started showing up in the student newspaper, which was edited by then-seminarian (now church theologian) Martin Marty. A good-humored librarian entered Bibfeldt's works in the card catalog, although they were always mysteriously out on loan. A glass case at the University of Chicago Divinity School now displays Bibfeldt memorabilia, including autographed photographs expressing esteem for Bibfeldt from such aficionados of theology as former Mayor Richard J. Daley, Lester Maddox, and the 1971 Playmate of the Year.

Bibfeldt is the master of Accommodation Theology. After reading Søren Kierkegaard's unyielding, classic volume on faith, *Either/Or*, Bibfeldt wrote a reply entitled *Both/And*. When the book received disparaging reviews, Bibfeldt offered a revision entitled *Either/Or and/or Both/And*. Some historians see Bibfeldt's pen behind President Dwight D. Eisenhower's famous statement that America has to be "founded on a deeply felt religious faith—and I don't care what it is." Seeking an audience beyond his Lutheran circle, Bibfeldt has offered advice to Roman Catholics, proposing, for example, that the Vatican "should keep celibacy, but make it a little easier for everybody."

> Theology, according to Bibfeldt, is "the art of making things come out right," and the task of theologians is to reconcile everything to everything else. . . . As an annual Bibfeldt lecturer has explained, the great scholar's method is thus "to affirm all propositions simultaneously, in the hope that some of them might be true and a few of them might even be popular." . . . Bibfeldt's coat of arms shows Proteus— the mythological figure who could change shapes at will—rampant on a weather vane. The motto is an old Spanish proverb: "I dance to the tune that is played."[2]

"I dance to the tune that is played." Many clergy have been doing that dance for so long that they have forgotten the tune that brought them into ministry in the first place. The truth is that the Theology of the Cross, Liberation Theology, Feminist Theology, and Womanist Theology, learned so often with zeal and enthusiasm in the seminary classroom, usually succumb after a few years of pastoral ministry into Bibfeldt's Theology of

Accommodation. Whether it is out of a neurotic need to please all sides and to be liked by everyone, or because of a calculated fear of alienating the key leaders and key givers of congregations, or simply due to timidity and cowardice, the clarity of conscience in clergy often gets blurred by acquiescence to accommodation.

Clergy are perceptive enough to know that the public arena can get rough and tumble. The public arena is where you can get crucified. And so clergy stay in the sanctuary where they are comfortable and where their status is secure. In what is probably an honest gesture, Willow Creek and other mega-churches have simply removed the cross as a symbol from their sanctuaries. Forget the public arena. It is easier to worship and adore the middle-class life of comfort and security.

Perhaps something worse than the Accommodation Theology keeps clergy and their churches in the sanctuary. This something worse is the civil religion that engages the public arena to promote, not the ethical imperatives of Jesus, but the enterprise of the nation. Some years ago I took a tour of the Pentagon. As we passed through the Chiefs of Staff corridor, I was startled to see a large painting that depicted a church sanctuary in which an athletic-looking couple and their two children were kneeling at the altar railing. To their right was a stained glass window in which an Air Force pilot stood beside his jet airplane dressed in battle fatigues. The caption of the painting was from the book of the prophet Isaiah: "'Whom shall I send, and who will go for us?' And I said, 'Here am I; send me!'"

I was at the Pentagon to fast and vigil with a group of religious resisters against the madness of nuclear build-up and militarism generated in that place. With us at the River entrance was a Japanese Buddhist monk who hour after hour solemnly beat his prayer drum. It was August 6, the anniversary of the dropping of the atomic bomb on Hiroshima. A woman pulled up in her station wagon to pick up her husband from work. "Jesus Is the Answer" was proclaimed on a bumper sticker on her car. Before she ascended the steps of the Pentagon, she pulled me aside and said, "What's your obligation to tell your Buddhist friend there about Jesus?" Indeed.

Churches that have been seduced by civil religion engage the public arena but usually do so to support capital punishment, military build-up, or other social policies that are punitive toward people in poverty, immigrants, and people of color. They are guided by servitude to the dominant culture, not by servanthood to the Sermon on the Mount. This response is nothing new. Historically, the church has often aligned itself with oppressive forces and crucified its Lord anew. Small wonder that many reflective persons would prefer to see the church stay in the sanctuary where it can remain irrelevant and do little harm.

None of these forces alter the summons of Jesus to the public arena. The Great Commission demands it. The Sermon on the Mount guides it. As St. Augustine says, "God has a work to do with us that cannot be done without us." This work of God with us has to do not only with the sanctification of our inner being but with the salvation history of the world. In fact, both are interrelated. Any sanctification that precludes involvement in the world must be rendered suspect. Any involvement in the world that disregards sanctification is dangerous. The activity of God in the public arena is incarnational and co-creational. God's work is done through human beings. There is no purity in this work, just as there is no purity in human beings. If the church awaits pure action, it will never act. If the church keeps one ear to the Sermon on the Mount and the other ear to the cries of a suffering humanity, perhaps it will learn to act in ways that contribute to God's salvation history. If not, God will find other servants than the church for the work that must be done. God's activity in the world is certainly not limited to what the church does or fails to do.

What is the nature of the church's work in the public arena? I recall meeting with a group of bishops and judicatory leaders in Erie, Pennsylvania, to encourage their support of an emerging congregation-based community organization affiliated with the Gamaliel Foundation. One of the bishops was resistant and suspicious. He said, "The role of the church in society is not to engage systemic injustice but to fill in the gaps." This view is, of course, the practical, working theology of most churches in the United States whose social ministry, if it exists at all, is devoted to food pantries, homeless shelters, or walk-a-thons to generate money for this or that cause.

Now clearly, some merit lies in such an approach. The Parable of the Last Judgment directs us to a charity based on personalism and compassion. The hungry must be fed. The homeless must be sheltered. The works of mercy are central to the teachings of Jesus. When we engage in a personal ministry of mercy, we have an opportunity to learn from those who suffer. We move beneath tidy statistics to the complexities of the human dimension. We begin to see how systems are designed to benefit the prosperous and to keep the poor down. Our prejudices and false assumptions are challenged. We learn to see the world in a new way—from the perspective of those at the bottom. This view can be quite threatening to us. We cling to our fragile security and try to preserve a safe distance.

One rainy day in Jersey City, I sat in the parsonage emotionally fatigued. The doorbell rang. I peered through a front window and saw that it was Clarkie, one of the street alcoholics I had helped from time to time. I didn't want to deal with him. So I ignored the doorbell. Clarkie kept pushing that button. So I went to the back of the house to get myself a cup of coffee and to hide deeper in the parsonage. Clarkie went around to the back of the house and knocked on the back door. He looked through a window and saw me. Seeing him see me, I reluctantly opened the door. Before he could say a word, I said, "Clarkie, I can't help you out today. I don't have any money or food to give you [a transparent lie]." "I don't want any money or food," said Clarkie. "I just need to talk and have you pray for me."

What could I say? I let him in. We sat in the living room. Clarkie's head was bandaged. He said that two days ago one of his street buddies had hit him over the head with a board and robbed him of all he had—27 cents. The police had taken him to the hospital. He was just released this morning. "Why would my friend do that to me?" Clarkie asked. We talked a little longer. We prayed. Clarkie asked for a Bible. I gave him one. That's all he asked for. A few days later I learned that Clarkie died from a brain hemorrhage the day after I saw him.

The works of mercy reveal our own need for mercy, our own limitations, our own poverty of spirit. Benefit can be found in these revelations.

On the other hand, the works of mercy are considerably limited if they are done without regard to systemic injustice. Society is pleased to have the church exhaust itself in being merciful toward the casualties of unjust systems. I recall a friend of mine who was asked to go to Guatemala to work with homeless children. At first, she was drawn by compassion to accept this offer. But then she learned that this charitable effort was being funded by the ruling families of Guatemala. The children being served were those whose parents had been disappeared and murdered by right-wing death squads who were supported by the ruling families. The wealthy wanted to assuage their guilty consciences by providing for children whom they had helped to orphan. The director of the shelter for children made it clear to my friend that any critique of this arrangement would be unacceptable.

This prevailing protocol surrounds much of what passes for charity in the United States. Those providing direct services to the poor are often reliant on the financial contributions of wealthy donors. Providers cannot risk offending such donors by asking hard questions or challenging unjust systems. The Christians who are so generous with food baskets at Thanksgiving or with presents for the poor at Christmas often vote into office politicians whose policies ignore or crush those living in poverty. A kind of pseudo-innocence permeates this behavior. It makes me feel good to be charitable, but I don't really want to understand or challenge the systemic causes of poverty.

The works of mercy can degenerate into merciless works when wrought, not by a doer of good, but by a do-gooder. The do-gooder operates out of condescension. The do-gooder is always "for" the other and not "with" the other. The do-gooder seeks to help while secretly despising the one who is helped. The do-gooder needs the powerlessness of the other in order to feel powerful. The do-gooder basks in the gratitude of those who are helped. The do-gooder needs to be needed. The self-identity and sense of importance of the do-gooder are enhanced by his or her role in tending to the misery of others. The do-gooder gathers tragic stories to tell to entranced audiences at social gatherings. The do-gooder has much at stake in keeping things as they are. If the powerless were empowered, what would the do-gooder do?

Churches that are not enthralled by a do-gooder mentality often turn to advocacy. They are at the side of the one in need. They speak on behalf of the powerless. They enter into the maze of systems. Here pastors and lay leaders learn what it means to deal with landlord-tenant complaints, to seek treatment for a drug addict, to appeal a denial for SSI, to advocate for a child in the court system. These actions are all well and good. Advocates with savvy who know how to work their way through systems are a great resource. But such advocates at best bring about exceptions to the rule. They are able to create individual justice for the moment but lack the power to create the systemic justice that is lasting. Advocates do not change systems.

While pastoring in Jersey City, I was approached by an African American woman whose brother, a college student, had been brutally beaten by two police officers after being pulled over for a minor traffic violation. I met with the young man and became convinced of the credibility of his claim, which was strengthened by the racist, brutal reputations of these two officers. We met with investigators from the Internal Affairs Unit of the police department. The young man secured a lawyer. I enjoined the support of the local branch of the NAACP, since I was on its executive committee. The commissioner for the Jersey City Human Rights Division, a local pastor, offered his support. We met with two sympathetic aldermen, who recommended that we seek a public investigation into police brutality in Jersey City. They proposed introducing a resolution to this effect at the next meeting of the city council.

We contacted clergy and interested citizens. Strong advocacy seemed to be shaping up, but in reality we had no organizational base for our efforts. When the day came for the resolution to be introduced at the city council, the only persons who showed up in support of the resolution were myself, the immediate family of the young man, and the Human Rights commissioner. The police were much more effective. They had seventy-five police officers present carrying signs condemning any investigation into police brutality and shouting at me when I rose to address the city council. Seeing the opposition, the Human Rights commissioner told me that he had to "get back to work" and quickly exited the chambers. One of the aldermen had the courage to introduce the resolution. It was soundly defeated.

The political pressure generated by this advocacy was helpful to the victim of police brutality. His attorney was able to secure a favorable settlement from the city with considerable ease. But the advocacy effort, devoid of any real organizational base and strategy, was ineffectual in creating any substantial change in police behavior. An individual was helped. The system remained intact.

Action by resolution is another means by which some churches seek to engage the public arena. These resolutions may be heatedly debated on the convention floors of denominational assemblies. The problem is that such resolutions usually state what others should do, whether it be government or corporate America, without setting forth what the church will do. Little in the way of conscience or courage comes out of these resolutions. They normally hold no substance, no leverage, no strategy beyond having a bishop or presiding church official communicate to some government agency the intent of the resolution. With much posturing and speechifying, the garrulous clergy pride themselves on accomplishing something when their resolution has passed. But it has cost them nothing other than some hot air, and it has won them nothing. Unless a public policy resolution is attached to a judicatory budget, it usually matters little how the vote goes.

The same holds true for church social statements. Church bureaucrats, theologians, bishops, task forces, and commissions study, research, deliberate, and debate this or that social issue. Preliminary drafts are disseminated for public reaction. Revisions are made. Considerable resources of time, money, and energy are squandered in the preparation of thick documents that few people bother to read. Perhaps their primary value is in being used as references for citation in future church documents. All too often the church deludes itself into imagining that it has now taken a bold and courageous stand.

For people of faith who are alert to the limitations of direct service, advocacy, church resolutions, and church social statements, a vital alternative remains. Congregation-based community organizing offers a faithful and effective vehicle for seeking justice in the public arena.

CHAPTER 4

Congregation-Based Community Organizing

> "When Moses' father-in-law saw all that he was doing for the people,
> he said, 'What is this that you are doing for the people? Why do you
> sit alone, while all the people stand around you from morning until
> evening? . . . What you are doing is not good. You will surely wear
> yourself out, both you and these people with you. For the task is too
> heavy for you; you cannot do it alone.' . . . So Moses listened to his
> father-in-law and did all that he had said. Moses chose able men from
> all Israel and appointed them as heads over the people, as officers over
> thousands, hundreds, fifties, and tens." (Exod. 18:14, 17-18, 24-25)

Congregation-based community organizing has its roots in the organizing principles first forged by Saul Alinsky in the Back of the Yards
neighborhood of Chicago in the 1930s. Upton Sinclair described the
grim social conditions of this community in his classic book *The Jungle*.
Early efforts to improve these conditions began with the assumption that
something was wrong with the people in this impoverished neighborhood and that solutions were to be discovered through the infusion of a
range of social services. Alinsky, a radical thinker from the University of
Chicago, took a different approach. He concluded that the problem was
not with the people in the community but rather with the outsiders who
profited from and abused the community. The stockyards polluted the air
and the sewer systems. The stockyard workers were exploited. A corrupt
political machine controlled by City Hall did not represent the interests
of the people. The police had mob connections. The schools, starting
with the assumption that "those" children could not learn, did not teach.

In 1938, Alinsky organized the Back of the Yards Neighborhood Council, a power base for ordinary citizens to participate in the social, political,
and economic decisions affecting their lives. The motto of the Back of
the Yards Neighborhood Council was: "We shall decide our own destiny."
The assumption was that if the institutions representing the people of the
community came together, they could exert enough influence to control

the political and economic decisions shaping the life of the community. Bringing together unions, civic organizations, ethnic clubs, sports teams, business groups, and churches, the Council proved through its actions and achievements that Alinsky's analysis was correct and that his approach was effective.

Alinsky was brilliant, brash, and often abrasive. He was skilled at inflating his success stories and promoting himself. He scorned moral suasion, scoffed at reconciliation, and gave overriding value to expediency. But he also laid the groundwork for a new way of creating true democracy in America. His methodology has had a major impact on hundreds of communities throughout this country. Cesar Chavez, mentored by Alinsky, began his organizing in this tradition.

Although the practice and principles of congregation-based community organizing have been heavily influenced by Alinsky, most laity and clergy engaged in these organizations have never read any of his writings, and many have never heard of him. A more direct connection is felt to the civil rights movement and to the work of Dr. Martin Luther King, Jr. Particularly for people of faith, Dr. King is viewed as God-sent, as a prophet whose vision and charisma mobilized tens of thousands into the courageous struggles of the civil rights movement. Dr. King's consistent summons to nonviolence, to conscience, to the kingdom values of Jesus, to passionate prayer joined to civil disobedience, speaks directly to the hearts of believers. The historic success of the civil rights movement encourages those who still hope that the church can signify the kingdom of God in an oppressive society.

Congregation-based community organizing joins the values and principles of Dr. King to the methodology of Saul Alinsky. Here we have a creative, often uneasy tension between faithfulness and effectiveness, morality and expediency, conscience and compromise, the prophetic and the practical, the world as it should be and the world as it is. There are those who cannot handle this tension. It seems to be an unholy alliance. But it is within this tension that a creative and intriguing experiment is under way in scores of cities throughout the United States as people of faith are organized to live out their values in the public arena in the pursuit of social justice.

Congregation-based community organizing is an emerging phenomenon. About twenty-five years ago, the Catholic Campaign for Human Development (CCHD), the primary social justice funding vehicle of the Roman Catholic Church in the United States, awarded its first grant to a congregation-based community organization. In 1999, CCHD funded eighty-nine such organizations. Four national networks of congregation-based community organizations are active in the United States: the Gamaliel Foundation, which is based in Chicago; the Industrial Areas Foundation (IAF), also based in Chicago; the Pacific Institute for Community Organization (PICO), which is based in Oakland; and the Direct Action and Research Training Center (DART), which is based in Miami. A conservative estimate is that the member churches in the congregation-based community organizations of these four national networks comprise more than 3 million Christians.[1]

In the 1970s, the Industrial Areas Foundation (IAF) began to use Alinsky's organizing principles to form congregation-based community organizations. One of their stellar organizations, East Brooklyn Congregations (EBC), received national attention with its development of the Nehemiah Project, which constructed more than 2,200 affordable, single family homes in a previously devastated section of Brooklyn. The IAF organizations in Texas brought together as many as 10,000 people for statewide action on education issues and have won $100 million in state funds to subsidize water supply and sewer development in poor subdivisions along the Mexican border. With sixty-five affiliated organizations across the United States, the IAF is the largest of the four national networks.

PICO began in 1972 with organizing efforts in Oakland, California. Now operating in ten states and with thirty-two organizations, PICO has an impressive track record. In California, PICO won a $50 million increase in funding for community clinics. In Santa Clara County, California, PICO secured $14 million annually from tobacco settlement funds to guarantee health coverage for 68,000 uninsured children in Santa Clara County.

Formed in 1981, DART has eighteen organizations in six states. DART victories include $7.25 million from the Florida state legislature for increasing the use of Direct Instruction in elementary schools across the state and $20 million for an affordable housing trust fund in Columbus, Ohio.

The Gamaliel Foundation has enjoyed the fastest growth of the four networks. Formed in 1986, Gamaliel's network includes forty-five organizations in fifteen states and three organizations in South Africa. Gamaliel victories include a $1 billion agreement with banks in Chicago for home mortgage loans in low-income neighborhoods, $60 million from the

Minnesota state legislature to fund brownfield cleanup in older sections of Minneapolis and St. Paul, $50 million from the Michigan state legislature for public transportation, and $30 million from the Wisconsin state legislature to reduce student-teacher ratios in Milwaukee's public schools.

The Gamaliel Foundation has the distinction of being the only network with an organized and staffed national Clergy Caucus. The Gamaliel National Clergy Caucus (GNCC) has a structure of elected officers and regional representatives who meet quarterly to plan annual theological training for clergy, to share strategies for strengthening local clergy caucuses, to promote the interests of congregations and clergy within the network, to facilitate network expansion, and to deepen judicatory relationships.

Congregation-based community organizations are formed in much the same way in each of the networks. Usually a few visionary clergy or bishops invite a network to their city to explore the possibility of organizing. An organizer is sent to meet with interested leaders. A presentation by the organizer covers the basic principles and methodology of organizing. If the conversation gets serious, a relationship between local congregations and the network begins to develop. A sponsoring committee is formed with three specific tasks: raising money (normally $150,000), recruitment of dues-paying congregations (usually at least twenty), and training (sending significant numbers of leaders to the national weeklong or ten-day training of the network). At the onset, these tasks seem daunting. But networks know better than to respond to half-hearted commitments that will result in faltering, weak organizations. The point is to build power organizations, and this goal requires organized money and organized people.

As a sponsoring committee completes its initial tasks, core teams in each member congregation are trained to do one-on-one interviews within their congregational community. The one-on-one is the basic tool of organizing for relationship building and for discerning self-interest. After thousands of these interviews have been completed, an issues assembly is conducted in which the interviewers share their findings in a process that democratically identifies issues of most concern to the congregants. Hundreds of important issues can be identified in any city. The point is to identify issues that address the self-interest of those who are part of the organizing effort and who will be asked to pay the cost of victory with their money, time, and action. Initially three or four issues are selected and task forces are formed to do research, power analysis, the shaping of a winnable issue, and proposed action. The sponsoring committee then holds a massive public meeting in which a thousand or more people come together to celebrate the formation of an organization and to announce its initial issues campaign. The sponsoring committee is phased out of existence. A new congregation-based community organization has been born. Dom Helder Camara, Brazilian Archbishop and champion of the poor, once said: "If I dream alone, it is only a dream. If we dream together, it is the beginning of reality." And so it is with the formation of congregation-based community organizations.

Each of the four national networks applies Alinsky's principles to faith-based organizing. These networks, operating in the major metropolitan regions of the United States, realize that in most low-income, urban areas, the church is the last remaining viable institution apart from gangs, organized crime, and taverns. Although some of these churches are otherworldly in their theology and detached from the social needs of their neighborhoods, or simply too small and fragile to make much impact, a sizable number of churches in any urban area are positioned to be recruited into the organizing enterprise. Metropolitan organizing also embraces those suburban congregations who realize that their future is linked to the future of the central city and who are willing to engage the public arena in the pursuit of justice.

Congregation-based community organizing is rooted in the local congregation. The local congregation is the building block of the organization. Organizing must be linked to the faith and values of the local congregation, to its self-interest, to its needs for leadership training, to the realities of its neighborhood. Organizers must be attentive to the particular ethos and character of the local congregation. The pastor must be drawn into the center of the organizing effort; otherwise, the congregation as a whole will likely remain on the periphery.

While congregation-based community organizations may have powerful congregations in their membership, invariably a number of member congregations struggle to remain viable. Roman Catholic and so-called mainline Protestant congregations in the inner city often have an aging membership, dwindling bank accounts, deteriorating buildings, dangerous neighborhoods, and demoralized leadership. A pastor in Cleveland, using a sports metaphor, stated that his congregation had experienced "twenty losing seasons in a row." Each year the congregation became numerically smaller, financial resources shrank, and the community around the church continued to deteriorate. In such cases, the concepts of organizing must be applied to the mundane realities of congregational life at the edge. When concepts such as self-interest, leadership training, empowerment, agitation, and relationship building are actually implemented, a new sense of vitality is experienced within the congregation. Stewardship, evangelization, worship, and mission are all invigorated. The fact is that congregation-based community organizing can strengthen the local congregation even as it engages the local congregation in the public arena.

One way to grasp the significance of congregation-based community organizing is to encounter its achievements. Jesus curses the fig tree that bears no fruit. Given that churches are notoriously fruitless when it comes to producing social justice, organizers must be blessed indeed with a charisma that flows directly from the Holy Spirit. For those within the church who long for the church "to set at liberty those who are oppressed," it is inspiring and encouraging to see the just fruits of congregation-based community organizing.

As a case in point, I offer the achievements of Milwaukee Inner-City Congregations Allied for Hope (MICAH), an affiliate of the Gamaliel Foundation. Incarnation Lutheran Church, the congregation that I serve in Milwaukee, was one of the founding members of MICAH in 1989. With a current membership of forty-six congregations interfaith, MICAH has emerged as a respected power organization in Milwaukee that is extending beyond the inner city to develop a metropolitan membership base. Here are some highlights of MICAH's achievements to date:

- Won passage of a city ordinance requiring that at least 14 percent of jobs in Department of Public Works contracts be set aside for unemployed residents of the central city of Milwaukee. The initial 14 percent requirement was later increased to 25 percent. This ordinance created hundreds of jobs for central city workers.
- Won passage of a city ordinance mandating that at least fifty abandoned houses be rehabbed annually for low-income housing.
- Beginning with a prayer vigil on October 14, 1993, at the site of the drive-by killing of twelve-year-old Monte Fuller, MICAH has conducted more than 500 prayer vigils at the sites of homicides in Milwaukee. For some families, it was the only prayer service offered for a slain loved one.
- Forged the Banking Campaign of MICAH, which involved 17 financial institutions in an aggregate commitment of $500 mil-

lion of central city lending over a five-year period. In cooperation with MICAH, lenders developed new marketing strategies, hired more minority loan officers, changed their way of viewing credit history and debt ratio, and responded favorably to MICAH's advocacy on behalf of many applicants who had originally been denied loans. At the end of five years, more than $700 million had been lent.

- After many other efforts failed, an all-night pray-in at the offices of the Milwaukee County Executive resulted in the restoration of $3.3 million in proposed cuts for drug treatment funding and an agreement not to go below this level of funding in subsequent budgets.

- Established a drug hot-line in cooperation with the Milwaukee Police Department, which has resulted in the closure of more than 350 drug houses in the City of Milwaukee.

- Won an agreement with Milwaukee County to fund an AODA intake and referral center at one of the MICAH churches as a means of assessing the availability and quality of drug treatment while providing a much needed service.

- Won passage of a city ordinance stiffening the penalties for negligent landlords, providing for ongoing monitoring of problem landlords, and increasing communication of tenant rights.

- Successfully pressured the Immigration and Naturalization Service (INS) offices in Milwaukee to expand their hours of operation, hire bilingual staff, and create easier access to information for immigrants seeking citizenship.

- Launched an Alternative Teacher Certification project in cooperation with area colleges and the Dorothy Danforth Compton Fellowship Program. To date about sixty-five minority persons, mostly second career, have been trained through this consortium to become teachers in the Milwaukee Public Schools system.

- Succeeded in getting the Fire and Police Commission to move its offices from the Safety Building to a neutral site so that citizens with complaints about police brutality may file these complaints without feeling the intimidation of a police presence.

- Entered into a partnership with Badger Mutual Insurance Company to create an affinity plan offering members of MICAH congregations a 10 percent discount on auto insurance. For central city residents, who have suffered under discriminatory rating territories by insurance companies, the plan has created a consumer awareness leading to personal savings ranging from a few hundred dollars to as high as $1,400 per year.

- Secured $7.5 million in state funding for drug treatment for uninsured addicts in Milwaukee County.

- Initiated and inspired a successful effort to win statewide funding for fifty-one additional SAGE schools in the Milwaukee Public Schools system. SAGE schools reduce the student-teacher classroom ratio to 15:1 in kindergarten through the third grade.

- Scores of actions at the core team level of MICAH congregations have resulted in victories against problem landlords, closure of drug houses, rehab of board-ups, better police protection, withdrawing the liquor license from a tavern that was a center for shootings and drug activity, creation of church-operated community development corporations, challenge of exorbitant interest rates of rental centers, and exposure of landlords who rent to drug traffickers.

- Leadership training for hundreds of members of MICAH congregations at the national, weeklong trainings of the Gamaliel Foundation, at the annual Gamaliel National Clergy Training, and at the local level. Such training has not only been essential for the effectiveness of MICAH but also for the strengthening of MICAH congregations.

All of these activities are notable, but how have the members of Incarnation Lutheran Church benefited from the involvement of our congregation in MICAH? Like many urban congregations, Incarnation has a history of direct service to its neighborhood through such programmatic ministries as an emergency food pantry, an after-school tutoring program, a summer youth program for neighborhood children, a parish nurse, a crisis fund, and a community development corporation. As worthy as these ministries are, none of them comes close to offering the empowerment, leadership development, and engagement in social justice that comes with being a part of MICAH.

When we used our MICAH core team in our annual stewardship drive to do the every-member visitation, the result was an actual increase of $10,000 in congregational giving (a substantial sum for a low-income congregation of modest size). Leadership training offered by Gamaliel at the national level and by MICAH at the local level has honed the skills of established leaders in the congregation and surfaced new leadership. Meetings are run more efficiently.

Leaders know better how to organize money, act according to authentic self-interest, and build healthy relationships with each other and with unchurched neighborhood residents. The congregation has more clarity about its mission in the neighborhood and in the city. The congregation has a larger sense of the church, working closely not only with other Lutherans but with Baptists, Pentecostals, Roman Catholics, United Methodists, Presbyterians, Quakers, and Episcopalians. Through the one-on-one interviewing process, a deeper sense of community has been created. A more dynamic relationship is nurtured between the Word of God proclaimed on Sunday and the actions of the congregation in the public arena during the week.

Under the direction of Doris Owens, an Incarnation leader with extensive relationships in the neighborhood of the church, our core team has designated a three-block radius around Incarnation as a Safe Zone. The core team, primarily comprised of neighborhood residents (about half of whom are members of Incarnation), takes action on drug trafficking, sanitation, abandoned vehicles, deteriorating properties, and other neighborhood issues. The core team also conducts one-on-one interviews in the congregation, identifies persons for leadership training, has representation on MICAH task forces, and produces turnout for MICAH actions and public meetings.

Some members of Incarnation have benefited directly from MICAH. Their stories offer a personal testimony to the ability of organizing to meet the self-interests of congregants.

Stephanie Roland, a bright young adult member of Incarnation, worked hard to get her teaching degree from the University of Wisconsin–Milwaukee. The congregation celebrated her achievement and was proud of her when she accepted her first assignment to teach at a public school in Milwaukee. One Saturday during the first semester of her teaching, Stephanie and her two little children went to visit her mother. Her mother had just had a heated argument with another tenant in the building. The son of the tenant then showed up with several of his friends. They spoke of killing Stephanie's mother. Noticing that the son was holding a revolver, Stephanie slammed shut the door of the apartment, threw her children beneath a bed, and called 911. The police arrived shortly and arrested the son of the tenant. He was charged with a felony and with violation of parole.

Given the volatility of the situation, Witness Protection recommended that Stephanie move from her apartment because the defendant's mother knew Stephanie's address. Stephanie moved. But Stephanie's sense of security was lost when she received a phone call one morning at the school where she taught. It was the defendant's mother, threatening to kill Stephanie if she testified against her son. Witness Protection offered no further support.

Stephanie met with me to discuss the moral dilemma she faced. Should she testify and risk her life or not testify and violate her moral obligation to justice? I asked her what would help. She said that if she knew that security was watching her in the parking lot at the school when she arrived in the morning and left at the end of the day, she would feel sufficiently confident to testify. The only place where she really felt vulnerable was in the parking lot at the school. But she had already discussed this with the school principal. Although the principal was empathetic and supportive, she could not get the central office administration to authorize the additional funding required to have security in the parking lot at the beginning and end of the day. She was already over budget. I suggested to Stephanie that our MICAH core team deal with this issue.

We contacted the MICAH lead organizer, Ana Garcia Ashley. She was able to arrange a meeting the next day with Howard Fuller, superintendent of the Milwaukee Public Schools (MPS). Dr. Fuller was gracious and attentive. Four hours after our meeting, I received a phone call from the director of security for MPS. He assured me that Stephanie would have a security guard in the parking lot of her school beginning the next day and continuing as long as Stephanie felt the need for protection. Stephanie testified against the assailant. He was convicted and sent back to prison. His mother's threats vanished after the trial.

Tamicka Grant was a sophomore at Greenfield High School when she needed the intervention of our MICAH core team. I had confirmed Tamicka the previous year. I saw great potential in her but also realized that she had an uphill struggle in life. Her mother was an addict. Her father was in prison the first ten years of Tamicka's life. Tamicka was being raised by her grandmother, Catherine Grant, an elder of our congregation whom I admire for her saintly compassion and generosity of spirit. Tamicka bussed each day to Greenfield High School in a south suburb of Milwaukee under a special desegregation agreement between Milwaukee and suburban school districts. One afternoon in the cafeteria, some "skin heads" in this predominantly white school began hurling racial epithets and food at Tamicka and several of her African American friends. A fight ensued. Teachers tried to stop the melee. The police were called on the scene. The skinheads were given a suspension of a few days. Tamicka was charged with assaulting one of the teachers who had intervened; she faced an expulsion hearing before the Greenfield School Board.

Catherine and Tamicka met with me to discuss the situation. Tamicka protested her innocence. We decided to raise the matter before our MICAH core team. The members decided to stand behind Tamicka, feeling that she was being scapegoated in a clearly racial incident. The media picked up on the story with extensive coverage on Milwaukee television stations and in the newspapers. The planning meetings of our MICAH core team were crowded and lively. The education task force of MICAH became involved. I received phone calls from parents of other African American students with stories of serious racial incidents in a number of suburban schools. My wife, Lynn, who is an attorney, agreed to offer legal representation for Tamicka at the expulsion hearing, although the decision to expel was a foregone conclusion—Tamicka was an African American teenager from Milwaukee facing an all-white, elected school board in suburban Greenfield on charges of assaulting a teacher.

The hearing began at 8 P.M. on a weekday evening and lasted until midnight. The hearing room was packed with members of Incarnation and other MICAH congregations. TV cameras covered the hearing live. The atmosphere was tense. In the summary statements, the attorney representing Greenfield thanked the audience for our composure. The school board's decision was as we expected. Tamicka was expelled. As we left the building, the mother of one of Tamicka's friends noticed squad cars in the parking lot with German shepherd dogs inside. This realization created quite a stir. The whole scene reminded many of the adults of their experiences growing up in the South.

The next morning I went to Catherine's home to visit Tamicka. I processed with her what had happened and then asked her what she had learned from her experience. I'll never forget what she said: "I learned that justice is not always served. I learned that I am not alone. And I learned that I am powerful." Not bad for a fifteen-year-old girl. You don't always have to win to win.

Ricardo and Annette Roberts approached me after five Milwaukee banks had denied their application for a home mortgage loan. The denials made no sense to me. Ricardo had been the manager of a clothing store for seventeen years. Annette had worked for years for a health insurance company. They were attractive, intelligent, church-going people. On the other hand, I knew that several national studies cited Milwaukee for its pattern of racial disparity in home mortgage lending. African American applicants were four times as likely to be rejected as white applicants regardless of income level.

Seeking to remedy the problem of racial disparity in home mortgage lending and the difficulties in obtaining loans in the inner city of Milwaukee, MICAH had formed a committee to begin a relationship with M&I Bank, the second-largest banking institution in Wisconsin. As chair of this committee, I suggested to Annette and Ricardo that we meet with officers of M&I to review their credit history and to see whether M&I would offer a loan. They agreed. We met with a vice president of M&I and one of its loan officers. Their credit history showed a few late payments. My wife and I had recently bought a house and had sailed through the loan application process despite the fact that we had shown a number of late payments and IRS-issued threats of seizure over the years because of my war tax resistance. When I mentioned this, the vice president of M&I admitted that when applications contain gray areas, the loan decision may be based on a "halo" effect. Apparently, my wife and I had such a "halo." He also felt that Ricardo and Annette, as active members of Incarnation, had one. We were encouraged.

Two days later I received a phone call from the vice president. Although M&I had decided to honor the loan application, the prime mortgage insurer would not. Without a 20 percent down payment and without prime mortgage insurance, M&I could not grant the loan. I was angry and frustrated. "This is not what MICAH has in mind for a relationship with M&I," I said. "As far as I'm concerned, we're through with M&I." I hung up the phone. Five minutes later, I received a phone call from Dennis Kuester, president of M&I. He was friendly and conversational, and he said that M&I would grant the loan by keeping it in their portfolio without requiring 20 percent down or prime mortgage insurance. Ricardo, Annette, and I were elated. They bought a home.

The committee that I chaired continued to work with M&I. But we were stunned a few months later (January 1993), when new federal data was published showing that M&I, like most Milwaukee lenders, continued to show a serious racial disparity in home mortgage lending. We felt as though we were being taken for a ride. MICAH leaders met with Dennis Kuester to express our conviction that the relationship now had to enter a new level. We would be holding an Economic Summit on January 14, the eve of Dr. King's birthday, at Calvary Baptist Church, the congregation pastored by MICAH's president, the Rev. James E. Leary. We wanted M&I to come to the summit and to announce its agreement to lend $50 million within the MICAH boundaries (Milwaukee's inner city) over the next five years. If M&I refused, MICAH would begin "to up the ante." (Our intent, never shared with M&I, was to have hundreds of people wrap a red ribbon around the downtown headquarters of M&I to highlight racial redlining and to begin a boycott.)

On January 14, Dennis Kuester stood before a packed church, the mayor of Milwaukee, and the media at Calvary Baptist and announced that M&I was pleased to agree to lend at least $50 million within the MICAH boundaries over the next five years. Reverend Leary then got up and announced that even though MICAH celebrated the commitment of M&I, what was really needed was an agreement with many lenders committing $500 million for the inner city of Milwaukee. The meeting was Spirit-filled and exciting.

The next morning I received a phone call from Dennis Kuester congratulating me on MICAH's achievement. He then began to speak of his deeply felt Christian faith and suggested that we consider forming a prayer group of a few MICAH pastors and business leaders. Given the deep prejudices I have held against wealthy people as a "radical" Christian, I felt resistance to this idea. I also feared being co-opted. But I knew that I needed to be liberated from my judgmental attitudes toward the rich. And so a monthly prayer breakfast began and included two bank presidents, several CEOs of businesses, Reverend Leary, myself, my bishop, and several other pastors. It continues to this day.

In the spring of 1993, Dennis Kuester and MICAH hosted a meeting with the presidents of sixteen banks to present MICAH's $500 million lending goal for the inner city of Milwaukee and to recommend specific lending goals for each bank. We were at the University Club, a meeting place for corporate Milwaukee. MICAH leaders, including me, felt uneasy and totally out of our element. But Kuester was a strong ally. The bankers listened and responded favorably. In the summer of 1993, at a public meeting of more than 1,000 people, MICAH heard sixteen additional banks agree to lending goals for the inner city of Milwaukee. I had the honor of presiding at this portion of the meeting and announcing the aggregate total: $503 million of lending within the inner city of Milwaukee over the next five years.

At a MICAH banquet in May 1998, we awarded a plaque to each of the participating lenders. Over a five-year period, these lenders had issued loans within the MICAH boundaries totaling more than $700 million, contributing substantially to a 35 percent increase in home values in Milwaukee's inner city.

One summer day in 1996, a member of Incarnation requested my help in securing residential drug treatment. The member was without health insurance and needed to access Milwaukee County's voucher program, which provides residential drug treatment for indigent, uninsured addicts. When I explored this option, I was shocked to learn from treatment providers that the County would probably eliminate this voucher program from its 1997 budget. For years MICAH had been protesting the County's steady reduction in drug treatment funding. Now it appeared that the County would totally abdicate its responsibility for providing the uninsured with drug treatment. It would be devastating for the inner city of Milwaukee where the primary cause of chaos and violence can be traced to drug addictions and drug trafficking. More than 80 percent of prisoners incarcerated in Wisconsin committed their crimes while under the influence of crack cocaine, alcohol, and/or other drugs.

At the next meeting of the MICAH Clergy Caucus, I related what I had heard about the County's intent to eliminate the voucher program. The clergy were alarmed and angry. They knew how deadly this decision would be for the people and neighborhoods of their congregations. They knew that effective pastoral ministry in the inner city requires a system of reliable referral to drug treatment. MICAH had been unable to stop the reduction in County funding for drug treatment over the years, and so we felt that we needed to escalate our action. We would meet with the County executive, and if he refused to block the elimination of the voucher program, we would conduct a pray-in. We would refuse to leave and risk arrest.

MICAH actions had never involved civil disobedience. It was new territory for many of the clergy and lay leaders. But everyone knew how high the stakes were. No one was willing to allow the voucher program to go under.

When MICAH staff tried to arrange for a meeting with the County executive, his secretary said that he was unavailable. Given the impending vote on the proposed budget by the Milwaukee County Board of Supervisors, we could not wait. And so early one afternoon, about 150 members of MICAH congregations rallied outside the county courthouse, which houses the offices of county government. Then about fifty persons, accompanied by TV cameras, went into the building, past the police, and into the reception area of the County executive's office. Within minutes we had a meeting with the County executive.

The room was packed and the tension was palpable. But the County executive stood his ground. The matter was out of his hands. He would not promise to block the elimination of the voucher program. At this point, we announced that some of us would be staying to pray. And that it would be a very long prayer. MICAH staff led others out of the room while fifteen clergy and lay leaders remained. We began to pray. Our prayer went through the afternoon and into the evening. Police sealed off the building and the floor that we were on. Several sympathetic County supervisors entered to strategize with us. The media was allowed in every hour or so to do live interviews for the news. But we were allowed to remain. Apparently, the County executive had decided not to have us arrested. That night the pray-in turned into a memorable snore-in.

In the morning a number of County supervisors met with us and assured us of their intent to block elimination of the voucher program. Feeling that we had accomplished what we could, we walked past the police and left the County executive's office. The media coverage was strong and supportive. The pressure on the County supervisors was substantial. In session and following a volatile debate, the County Board of Supervisors voted to restore the $3.3 million in proposed cuts for the voucher program and to set that amount as the minimal level of funding for the next three years. Since this action, several members of Incarnation have utilized the voucher program to secure residential drug treatment as part of their recovery from addiction.

These stories and many others like them from other MICAH congregations form an important part of the oral history of congregation-based community organizing in Milwaukee. Scores of congregation-based community organizations across the United States have their own oral histories. Each is powerful. Each is noteworthy. Each speaks not only of the effectiveness of organizing concepts and strategies but of the faith and theology that shape them. We will now consider some of the essential concepts of organizing and attempt to understand and interpret them theologically and from the perspective of faith.

"But you will receive power when the Holy Spirit has come upon you; and you will be my witnesses in Jerusalem, in all Judea and Samaria, and to the ends of the earth." (Acts 1:8)

"Then comes the end, when he [Christ] hands over the kingdom to God the Father, after he has destroyed every ruler and every authority and power. For he must reign until he has put all his enemies under his feet. The last enemy to be destroyed is death. For 'God has put all things in subjection under his feet.'" (1 Cor. 15:24-27)

Organizers tend to have a rather straightforward approach to power. They want power. They want the people with whom they work to have power. And they want to build power organizations. They see power as essentially neutral. It can be used in the service of justice or abused in the service of evil. They point to the fact that in Spanish the word for power is *poder*, which literally means "the ability to act" or "to be able." Organizers see power as what is needed to get things done. Power is needed to combat discrimination, to rebuild cities, to fight urban sprawl, to reduce drug trafficking, to improve school systems. If a person wants to make such changes in the public arena, then he or she must decide to become a power person connected with a power organization.

Organizers are usually impatient with the ambiguity that most people of faith have with power. They think that this ambiguity serves the interests of politicians and the wealthy who want the rest of us to think of power as bad so that we will not threaten their status and position. Public officials call themselves "servants" in order to make us think that servanthood, not power, is the operative force for change. Organizers make note of Rollo May's thesis in his book *Power and Innocence*, which claims that most people seek innocence to avoid the responsibility of power. They contend that those who avoid power out of fear of being corrupted are probably doing so to avoid the high cost of having power: conflict, controversy, ridicule, defeat. Those exercising such avoidance in order to remain "innocent" are making a virtue out of their cowardice. According to organizers, power does not corrupt; power attracts the corruptible. Good people sit on the sidelines, wrap themselves in virtue, and allow other people's values to dominate society.

Organizers know that power comes from essentially two sources: organized people and organized money. Political parties, unions, banks, corporations, and the media wield power because they have organized people and/or organized money. Congregation-based community organizations working in low-income neighborhoods may not be able to organize millions of dollars, but they can organize sufficient money to hire professional organizers and to be independent of governmental control. The greatest source of power for congregation-based community organizations rests in the large numbers of people that can be organized around issues that meet their self-interest. Organizers say that moral suasion does not create social change. Social change is the product of power applied effectively in the public arena.

Such clarity and conclusions about power seem to come so easily to organizers, but less so to most of the rest of us. Lord Acton's statement that "power tends to corrupt, and absolute power corrupts absolutely" speaks to our experience. One does not need to point to Hitler or Stalin or other demagogues as evidentiary examples of Acton's maxim. We see in urban America the human destruction caused by power brokers and power systems, drug kings and gang leaders, greedy landlords and corrupted officials, principalities and powers. We know firsthand the way that power can crush whatever is in the way of its self-interest.

Power in the real world is often the tool of evil. And so Paul envisions the eschatological destruction of power: "Then comes the end, when he [Christ] hands over the kingdom to God the Father, after he has destroyed every ruler and every authority and power. For he must reign until he has put all his enemies under his feet" (1 Cor. 15:24-25). William Stringfellow, always biblically wary of power, interprets Paul's vision as total and unequivocal. For Stringfellow, the reiterated use of "every" and "all" in Paul's reference to rebellious powers includes: ". . . all institutions, all ideologies, all images, all movements, all causes, all corporations, all bureaucracies, all traditions, all methods and routines, all conglomerates, all races, all nations, all idols."[1]

But powerlessness also corrupts. Powerlessness is also the tool of evil. The fruits of powerlessness are the loss of dignity and pride, the loss of hope, turning to drugs or alcohol or escapist religion, families in disarray, violent crimes as desperate reactions to life without the power to pursue dreams and aspirations. To the powerless, the Bible frequently promises power. The ascending Jesus promises his disciples that they will "receive power when the Holy Spirit has come upon you." Hannah (echoed in Mary's Magnificat) exults that her God "raises up the poor from the dust; he lifts the needy from the ash heap, to make them sit with princes and inherit a seat of honor" (1 Sam. 2:8).

And so people of faith often find themselves with ambiguous and conflicting feelings about power. We see that Scripture has no single word about power. It is dishonest to focus only on those biblical passages about power that serve our interests. We disdain the corrupting influence of power. But we equally disdain the corrupting influence of powerlessness. We hate how evil uses power to destroy people. But we also know that it takes power to rise up against such evil.

We find that we cannot run away from power once we take the ethical teachings of Jesus seriously. These teachings draw us into a life of compassion and righteousness that seeks justice. On an interpersonal level, perhaps we find no tension. We visit the sick and imprisoned, shelter the homeless, and feed the hungry without conflict. But what happens when we begin to analyze why people are imprisoned, homeless, hungry, poor in a society of immense wealth? We begin to thirst for justice. This thirst for justice leads us into the public arena. And there we learn rather quickly the truth of Frederick Douglass's maxim: "Power yields nothing without a struggle. It never has and it never will."

We who try to live by the Golden Rule, by the mandate to love the enemy, by the perfect demands of the Beatitudes, now find ourselves in power struggles where we may act as a group in ways that we would not act as individuals. We experience the distinction that Niebuhr wrote about in his classic work, *Moral Man and Immoral Society*. "As individuals, men believe that they ought to love and serve each other and establish justice between each other. As racial, economic and national groups they take for themselves whatever their power can command."[2] Niebuhr was right. A sharp distinction can be drawn between the moral and social behavior of individuals and that of social groups, and this distinction often draws those seeking social justice into collective political actions that might seem offensive to an individualistic ethic.

The teachings of Jesus in the Sermon on the Mount clearly enjoin his disciples to nonviolence, and those who claim to follow Jesus deny him when they turn the cross into a sword. But given the systemic violence that daily demeans the lives of the poor, social justice must be pursued passionately and vigorously. Actions forcing politicians, bankers, or systems to act justly are often coercive. Whether it be as sweeping as sanctions against apartheid in South Africa or as basic as a public demonstration against the inaction of an elected official, nonviolent action to create social change that is powerful is usually coercive. While commitment to nonviolence must be unwavering, no one can make honest claim to moral purity in the public arena. As Saul Alinsky said, "Every action on behalf of justice creates an injustice."

Amnesia must not be the cost of acting in the public arena. We remember who we are as Christians. And we act accordingly. I recall how Betty Smith, one of MICAH's leaders, lived out her faith in the public arena on an issue of jobs for the unemployed. Her committee had worked for a year on a proposed piece of legislation that would set aside 14 percent of jobs on all Department of Public Works contracts for unemployed residents of Milwaukee's inner city. After extensive negotiations with labor unions and with the Association of General Contractors, an inner-city alderman agreed to sponsor the legislation. But everything was moving intolerably slowly. Finally, at a public meeting of 1,200 members of MICAH congregations, at which the alderman and other public officials were present, Betty Smith gave a stirring speech calling for an end to stalling. She urged the alderman to act now. Feeling betrayed and publicly humiliated, the alderman stormed out of the meeting.

The next morning the alderman pushed the legislation through his committee while at the same time excoriating MICAH for attacking him. Betty Smith tried to reach him by phone all day to seek understanding and reconciliation. He refused to accept her phone calls. That evening, after work, Betty went to the alderman's home, sat on his porch, and waited two hours for his arrival. Seeking him out in this way, she was able to press for an honest and open conversation. The emotional wounds took a while to heal for our good alderman (who is, by the way, a most decent and honest person).

Betty Smith was not seeking moral purity in the public arena. She was seeking jobs for hundreds of unemployed people. She acted nonviolently at the public meeting, but her action was also sufficiently coercive to force the alderman to move the legislation. She acted as a Christian. Her concern was not only for the unemployed but also for the alderman. Her relentless efforts to seek reconciliation reflected the depths of her Christian faith.

Small wonder that many people of faith prefer to turn away from power and the public arena. It feels safer, holier, and more comfortable to operate in the realm of the individual and interpersonal. Everyone speaks well of the Christian who serves soup to the homeless or volunteers at a shelter. Unless, of course, that Christian begins to question why people are homeless. Dorothy Day said, "When I feed the hungry, they call me a saint. When I ask why people are hungry, they call me a Communist."

Jesus said, "Woe to you when the world speaks well of you." Jesus had enemies. Jesus was controversial. Jesus turned tables upside down and confronted principalities and powers. Obedience to Jesus and to our conscience takes us where we may prefer not to go. The geography of faith is treacherous and difficult. It engages us in the public arena and in the formation and wielding of power. We are inclined to resist this summons of the Spirit.

Some fear the added responsibility that comes with power. Already exhausted by the burdens and demands of life, they simply want some peace and quiet. They do not want to be drawn into organizing efforts that will add meetings, commitments, relationships, and actions to their busy lives. Some do not enter the public arena because they lack confidence in their own gifts and abilities. They hide from power because they lack the self-confidence necessary to exercise it.

Some prefer to surround themselves with dependent relationships, with people who come to them for handouts and hugs. They draw their sense of self-worth from the dependency of the needy upon them. They do not really want a power that will empower others. Such empowerment would threaten their superior position as charitable benefactor, as caregiver, as provider for the poor. It is much easier to convince suburban congregations to donate money and emergency food to inner-city parishes than it is to recruit suburban congregations into a metropolitan power organization where they will sit as equals at the table with inner-city church folk.

Some do not want power because they are stuck in a theology that is privatistic rather than communal, extraterrestrial rather than historical, spiritualized rather than incarnational. They would rather float a half-foot off the ground in cathartic, religious bliss than be grounded in the thorny struggle for justice. Their battle with the demonic is individualistic and tragic, defying St. Paul's admonition for the church to engage the demonic in principalities and powers.

Some want power but only for themselves and for their churches. The concept of shared power holds little appeal. They will not be involved in congregation-based community organizations unless *they* are in leadership positions, unless *they* are in front of the TV cameras, unless *they* are continually reminded by the organizers of their importance. Their churches are little kingdoms in which the pastor enjoys exalted status. Their turf is sanctified and glorified. Side deals are cut with politicians and business leaders. Meanwhile, the neighborhoods surrounding their churches go under.

All these reasons for not engaging power are expressions of our brokenness and fallen nature. None of these reasons is rooted in a valid, theological critique of power or in a faithful commitment to the Lord Jesus. And over against these reasons stands the biblical view of power that summons us to engage and to use power in ways that are creative, liberating, and life giving. We turn now to Holy Scripture.

"Once God has spoken; twice have I heard this: that power belongs to God" (Ps. 62:11). So speaks the psalmist. And so speaks a considerable portion of the Hebrew Scripture. According to Young's Concordance, no fewer than 117 references are made to power in the Old Testament reflecting twenty-eight Hebrew words. That the people of Israel had at least twenty-eight different words for the concept of power is itself instructive as to the central role of power in their life and theology. The heavy predominance of these references has to do with power that belongs to God, is exercised by God, or is delegated by God. Power is in fact seen to be a significant attribute of God, which is wielded for divine power and divine glory. Confessionally, Christians profess their belief "in God the Father Almighty, Creator of heaven and earth." We do not worship a god who is ineffectual, limited, or constrained. As Martin Luther King, Jr., sermonized: "Our God is able." We do not worship power, but we do worship a God who is powerful.

According to Kittel, the Old Testament view of power as wielded and directed by the will of a personal God acting in history is in contrast to the nature religions that viewed power as exercised through the impersonal forces of *mana* or *orenda*.[3] Unlike nature religions and their modern devotees in the New Age movement, those faithful to Hebrew Scripture believe in a God of history who uses power to exercise the divine will. The God of Israel controls nature and uses power over it for divine, historical purposes. For example, the song of Moses heralds God's power in drowning the armies of Pharaoh: "The floods covered them; they went down into the depths like a stone. Your right hand, O Lord, glorious in power—your right hand, O Lord, shattered the enemy" (Exod. 15:5-6).

This text and many others recounting the use of power to establish God's will in history support Karl Rahner's proposal that "[power] is of itself a gift bestowed by God and a charge imposed by God. It can of course be abused, it can of course do harm. . . . But it has this in common with everything created, everything that is not of God. . . . Of itself [power] is good."[4] When we use power according to God's purposes we underscore the inherent goodness of power and are the vehicles of God's will in history.

God is the source of power. To exercise power without attributing one's power to God as source is to blaspheme God and to risk divine wrath and judgment. Nebuchadnezzar was driven insane as punishment for boast-fully crediting himself instead of God for the majesty of his kingdom. "And the king said, 'Is this not magnificent Babylon, which I have built as a royal capital by my mighty power and for my glorious majesty?' While the words were still in the king's mouth, a voice came from heaven: 'O King Nebuchadnezzar, to you it is declared: The kingdom has departed from you! You shall be driven away from human society, and your dwelling shall be with the animals of the field. You shall be made to eat grass like oxen'" (Dan. 4:30-32).

Likewise, the Israelites are warned against amnesia or revisionist mem-ory concerning the source of their prosperity. "Do not say to yourself, 'My power and the might of my own hand have gotten me this wealth.' But remember the Lord your God, for it is he who gives you power to get wealth, so that he may confirm his covenant that he swore to your ances-tors, as he is doing today" (Deut. 8:17-18).

Those who exercise power through congregation-based community organizing do well always to recognize the ultimate source of power. It is biblically insufficient for us to state that power comes from organized people and organized money. We must predicate such a statement with the faith claim that power belongs to God and comes from God. We are not protected from misuse and abuse of power by making such a faith claim. But if we do not, we are more than likely to abuse the power that has been entrusted to us by God.

People of faith are as vulnerable to the self-aggrandizing seductions of power as anyone else. In fact they may be more vulnerable if they insist on concealing their self-seeking impulses beneath the veil of religiosity or in making a *Gott mit uns* claim. As evidenced by the blood bath of religious conflict in the world today and throughout history, nothing may be quite as dangerous as blind faith combined with blind power.

The central power action of God in the Hebrew Scripture is the Exodus event. Norman Gottwald, in his monumental book *The Tribes of Yahweh*, convincingly demonstrates that the concept of Yahweh as a god who delivers from oppression was introduced first among a group of militarized escapees from Egypt under the leadership of Moses.[5] What Gottwald calls the Moses group spearheaded a rural coalition of peasants against the hated regimes of the city-states of Canaan, sometimes in alliance with the oppressed inhabitants of those cities.

The Canaanite peasants suffered from heavy taxation and forced labor under a ruling class of warriors and bureaucrats in the city-states who were themselves subordinate to the pharaohs of Egypt. With its belief in Yahweh as deliverer, the Moses group offered the spiritual inspiration for a coalition of revolt. What emerged was an Israelite society that carried antifeudal, anti-imperialist bias for the next two centuries and offered an egalitarian, extended-family, tribal community that lasted until the monarchies of Israel.

Those who are faithful to the God of Moses seek to use power in the pursuit of a society that is truly liberated. Only more bondage comes from simply exchanging one form of domination for another. If people of faith are to be inspired to enter the struggle for liberation, they need to be offered a vision of God as liberator. All too often, oppression is bolstered by oppressive religion. Liberation, for people of faith, must entail a view of God who is in solidarity with the oppressed, who seeks their liberation, who imparts a revelatory vision of a liberated world, and who instills in them the power requisite to strive toward that vision. For Christians, such a God is revealed in the person of Jesus the Christ. A cursory view of the New Testament shows us the prevalence of expressions of power and the centrality of power in the life of Jesus.

"For I am not ashamed of the gospel; it is the power of God for salvation to everyone who has faith" (Rom. 1:16). So says St. Paul. And so says a considerable portion of the New Testament. The conception of power in the Greek New Testament centers around the usage of two key words: *dynamis* and *exousia*. According to Walter Wink, *exousia* occurs 102 times in the New Testament and "usually bears the sense of the right or authorization to exercise power."[6] *Dynamis*, which occurs in the New Testament seventy-seven times, has the basic meaning of "being able" or having the capacity to act or to exercise force. In the Synoptic Gospels, the miracles of Jesus are often called *dynameis*, powerful acts, an interesting juxtaposition of pastoral healing and prophetic power. The power of God in the New Testament is given fullest expression in the life, person, death, resurrection, and second coming of Jesus the Christ.

The power of God at work in Jesus begins with what St. Paul calls his *kenosis*, his self-emptying, his willingness to relinquish his divine state in order to take on the form of a slave, being born in human likeness (Phil. 2:5-10). The point here is not that Jesus abandons power or condescends to enter our suffering as an act of divine commiseration, rather that God in Jesus enters into the human condition to set us free from bondage to sin and death, to release power within us that we might break the chains of oppression and be liberated. As J. Deotis Roberts says, ". . . God enters into self-limitation in order to share power with human beings and in order to grant us freedom of selfhood and the responsibility of persons."[7]

The self-limitation of God in the *kenosis* of Jesus the Christ is a means of our salvation and a vehicle for distributing the power of God throughout the community of believers. The *kenosis* is an act of solidarity that puts to rest any false notions of God as a deity who uses his power to rule through fear, through domination, through subjugation. This consideration is critical for those who are weary of authoritarian religion rooted in the conception of God as an all-powerful Father who demands submission. And so, as expressed by Dorothee Soelle:

> If God cannot give up his power, we cannot trust him. If he doesn't want our liberation and our self-determination, then he is no better than, at most, a liberal capitalist. The God whom we need is not a private owner. There is only one legitimation of power, and that is to share it with others. Power which isn't shared—which, in other words, isn't transformed into love—is pure domination and oppression.[8]

The *kenosis* of Jesus the Christ inspires a community in which hierarchy is abandoned and power is shared. Outdated styles of community organizing, remnants of which are still alive and well today, are *macho* in their character, without any particular self-critique, domineering, and structurally shaped to imitate corporate America. Congregation-based community organizing must seek shared-power, an egalitarian mutuality, and a deeper faithfulness to the values of Jesus. We need a relational power that comes from collective interaction and is genuinely democratic in process. We need an integrative power that seeks win-win victories. We need power that is rooted in love to lead us to justice. Devoid of love, power will bring us only another form of tyranny.

During his wilderness testing, Jesus resists Satan's false expressions of power: the use of power to betray spiritual commitment for the sake of material need; the use of power to build empire and pay homage to the demonic; the use of power to ensure miraculous intervention and to abandon the cross as consequence of prophetic action. After faithfully resisting each temptation to abuse power, ". . . Jesus, filled with the power of the Spirit, returned to Galilee" (Luke 4:14). Jesus does not turn away from power in the desert testing. He turns away from the abuse of power and returns in the power of the Spirit.

This Spirit power is critically divergent from the abusive power exercised by oppressive earthly rulers. The Spirit power of Jesus is characterized by healing (Luke 5:17; 8:46), humility (John 13:3-17; Matt. 18:4), shared wealth (John 6:1-14; Luke 19:8-9; Acts 2:46), and nonviolence (Matt. 5:21-22, 38-40, 43-44).

Organizers teach strategic principles of power. And we are grateful for that. We need to learn how to organize money and people in order to build an organization powerful enough to achieve justice in the public arena. We need to learn how to do power analysis, how to conduct one-on-one interviews, how to cut issues, how to agitate. But we must not sacrifice the power of our principles. We seek healing, shared power, shared wealth, nonviolence, radical community. Our tactics must exert power in ways that will bring both physical and spiritual liberation. We need both: the principles of power and the power of principles.

To exercise the principles of power without the power of principles leads to tyranny. To live out the power of principles without the principles of power leads to sentimentality. Together the principles of power and the power of principles can lead us to justice

If we do not want to add to the confusion and chaos of the public arena, then we need to tend to our souls. On one occasion when Elizabeth McAlister was jailed for an act of civil disobedience, she found herself threatened by violent cellmates. She wrote in a letter to me that they were "striking matches off their private hells." That image has stayed with me. If we seek to exercise power in the public arena but do not take time for inner reflection, for prayer, for the healing of our souls, then our actions will be fueled by our inner hells. Again, we see the model we need in Jesus, who is so often to be found alone in prayer, holding action and reflection in perfect balance.

Gregory Galluzzo, executive director of the Gamaliel Foundation, once wrote in a memo to his senior staff: "We have erred in the past by concentrating mainly about our power in the public arena. Organizing is more correctly about the power people must possess at the center of their being that enables them to be self-directed people. Socrates talked about the tragedy of the unexamined life. . . . Very few people in our society have the courage to begin to examine their lives and take control of them."[9] The inner journey is critical for confronting those demons that assert our inadequacies and our unworthiness, that prevent us from acting powerfully on our convictions and values, that keep us from experiencing the power of the Spirit.

The communal journey is also critical. We cannot discover God's power alone. We need the community to challenge us, to encourage us, to summon forth our gifts, to fire our passion, to remind us of our calling. The community nurtures our discovery of the purpose and meaning of our lives. The community agitates us in the spirit of Marianne Williamson (quoted by Nelson Mandela in his inaugural speech):

> . . . our deepest fear is not that we are inadequate. Our deepest fear is that we are powerful beyond measure. It is our light, not our darkness, that most frightens us. We ask ourselves, Who am I to be brilliant, gorgeous, talented, fabulous? Actually, who are you not to be? You are a child of God. Your playing small does not serve the world. There's nothing enlightened about shrinking so that other people won't feel insecure around you. We are all meant to shine, as children do. We were born to make manifest the glory of God that is within us. It's not just in some of us; it's in everyone.[10]

We need the community as well because we are battling principalities and powers, wickedness in high places. On our own we would be ineffectual, co-opted, or crushed. As a community, we experience a power that is greater than the sum of its parts. Within the community, we discover gifts, abilities, and power that we did not realize we had. As a community, we are emboldened and empowered to take stands and engage in struggles that we would not conceive of doing on our own.

The community of believers draws its power from God and trusts the power of God to lead toward victory. That victory may take the form of tentative triumphs within history or it may take the form of courageous faithfulness in the face of the cross. The community stands firm as it opposes the powers of evil because it believes in the One who could not be defeated even by death. Faith in the power of Christ's resurrection prevents the community from yielding to defeat of spirit or cynicism because it knows that, eschatologically, evil will be totally vanquished by God.

The faithful community experiences power rooted in love and resulting in justice. To be part of such a community is an honor and a powerful blessing. It is the experience of congregation-based community organizing.

CHAPTER 6

Self-Interest

"'So come, I will send you to Pharaoh to bring my people, the Israelites, out of Egypt.' But Moses said to God, 'Who am I that I should go to Pharaoh, and bring the Israelites out of Egypt?'" (Exod. 3:10-11)

"Then he said to them all, 'If any want to become my followers, let them deny themselves and take up their cross daily and follow me.'" (Luke 9:23)

Organizers say that the civil rights victories of the 1960s were the result, not of impassioned moral suasion, but of a convergence of self-interests. The self-interest of the African American community was clear. Thousands were prepared to go to jail, and some were even willing to face death in order to secure basic human rights. Northern liberal politicians wanted to get elected. Businesspeople wanted to protect their economic investments. Government could not endure ongoing, massive social unrest. The media had gripping, valuable stories to broadcast. The integrity and status of church leaders were at stake. These self-interests were brilliantly drawn together by the leadership of the civil rights movement to create historic, progressive, social change.

The public arena is a place where deals are continually being cut by corporate executives, politicians, labor unions, and community organizations on the basis of self-interest. Power brokers do their homework and establish relationships; they understand the self-interests of the parties with whom they are negotiating.

Government has the power to organize people through force, violence, money, bribery, and propaganda. Organizers organize people around self-interest. They claim that the concept of self-interest is necessary to understand and to embrace if one is to think clearly and to act directly in the public arena.

Church people, trained in the art of destructive self-denial, tend to identify self-interest with selfishness and thus see self-interest negatively as implying self-centeredness, egotistical behavior, narcissism, and disregard for others. Organizers view self-interest differently. They see it as a relational concept to be distinguished from the nonrelational concepts of selfishness and selflessness.

Selfishness is egocentric, self-obsessed, small-minded, neglectful of others, and greedy. The selfish person is emotionally truncated, antisocial, and incapable of developing genuine relationships. We are clear about the deficiency of people who act selfishly. No one wants to be around them.

We are less clear about selflessness. "He never thinks of himself" is, after all, widely considered to be a compliment. We consider selfless people to be saintly, humble, kind, loving, and generous. But we also do not admire a human doormat. "She lets others walk all over her" is a derogatory statement. So also is the observation: "He doesn't have a clue who he is" or "She has no idea what she wants in life." In reality, say organizers, selfless people tend to be perpetual victims and/or do-gooders who operate on the basis of manipulation and do not know how to create mutuality in their relationships.

Organizers view self-interest as the only true way of relating to another person because self-interest respects the two sides of the relationship. Selfishness denies the "other" in the relationship. Selflessness denies the "self" in the relationship. Self-interest honors both the "self" and the "other" in the relationship. Organizers say that to know your self-interest, to declare your self-interest, and to act on your self-interest is an act of political courage.

Self-interest may be short term or long term. The need for a job, for emergency food, for a safe environment for one's children, for quality education, for drug treatment, for reelection, for compliance with Community Reinvestment Act (CRA) requirements are all examples of short-term self-interest. Long-term self-interest operates on a deeper level and connects with one's values, one's faith, one's search for meaning and fulfillment in life. Neither the short-term nor the long-term self-interest of another person is to be presumed. Such knowledge flows from conversation rooted in relationship.

Knowledge of one's own self-interest also cannot be presumed. For many of us, the identification of our self-interest is an awkward and clumsy process. Perhaps we received clear messages in childhood that what we wanted did not matter, that in fact we did not matter. We grew so accustomed to this denigration of our self that we now have difficulty really knowing what we want or who we are. Many women were taught from

childhood on to place the needs of men before their own needs. Many
church people were taught that self-denial (not in the communitarian
sense of Jesus but in a neurotic sense) is essential to being a Christian. For
such people to learn their self-interest requires considerable reorienta-
tion, introspection, dialogue, and agitation.

The discovery, identification, and projection of one's self-interest is an
act of courage. The knowledge of another's self-interest and the decision
to act in honor of that self-interest are deeply relational. Such is the
insight and experience of organizers.

Self-interest is clearly a key concept for congregation-based community organizing. And yet it is also a troubling concept for those clergy and
lay leaders who feel that self-interest is antithetical to the self-denial mandated by their Lord Jesus in the summons to cross bearing in Luke 9:23.
If we are called to deny ourselves, then isn't it wrong to organize around
self-interest? Doesn't this act simply inflate the ego, exalt the self, and
lead us down a false path?

The summons of Jesus to self-denial seems on the surface to be dia-
metrically opposed to self-interest. And those Christians in the pulpit and
in the pew who live theologically on the surface have mastered the art of
self-denial. Their lives have become one long sacrifice. Clergy often
become so driven by the desire to be of service to others that they are in
constant disservice to themselves. Many pastors are addicted to work and
to the praise of their congregants, without any truly intimate relationships, rarely at home with their families. My first marriage ended in
divorce, in part because of my habitual "self-denial" as a pastor. I allowed
the church office to be in the front room of the parsonage. I welcomed
street alcoholics at the front door and the homeless into a spare bedroom.
At one point I invited a violent ex-con who had violated his parole to hide
out for several weeks in the parsonage. I thought I was denying myself
and taking up the cross. My wife had a more realistic appraisal of what
was going on. She left and stayed away until my guest was gone.

When we go beneath the surface, we see that all three Synoptic
Gospels (Matt. 16:24; Mark 8:34; Luke 9:23) place the primary saying of
Jesus about self-denial in the context of the first prediction of Jesus' own
suffering and death. Christian self-denial is to be understood as participation in the cross of Christ, the vehicle of our salvation and liberation. To
deny the self in this context is to deny the false self that is afraid of life,
afraid of death, afraid of taking any risks for one's values and beliefs. To
deny the self is to deny that within us which prefers the comfort of secu-

rity to the cross of freedom. To deny the self is to deny that within us which prefers always to save one's life even if it means losing one's soul in the process. To deny the self is to deny the individualistic and privatistic impulses within us that block us from engaging in community.

Jesus also summons us to love our neighbor as we love ourselves (Matt. 19:19, as in Lev. 19:18). Self-love is implied, assumed, and affirmed. Any expression of self-denial that reflects self-hate is thus unbiblical. In fact the self-denial to which Jesus calls us is the highest expression of self-love because the self-denial of the cross leads to the deepest experience of life and to the fullest imaginable self-fulfillment. The self-denial to which Jesus calls us invites us to live as fully and as freely as he lived. Such self-denial leads to self-discovery rooted in relationship with others and with God. It is the highest form of self-interest.

We need to distinguish self-interest from self-seeking activities that lead us down a false, privatistic path. A reference from Dante's *Inferno* may be helpful in this regard. With Virgil as his guide, Dante approaches the Gates of Hell and there he sees a grim sign that reads: "I am the way into the city of woe. I am the way to a forsaken people. I am the way into eternal sorrow. Abandon all hope ye who enter here." At the entrance to Hell, Dante sees the souls of those who in life were neither for good nor for evil but only for themselves. Eternally unclassified, they race round and round pursuing a wavering banner that runs forever before them through the dirty air. As they sinned, so are they punished. In life they took no sides, therefore they are given no place. As they pursued the ever-shifting illusion of their own advantage, changing their courses with every changing wind, so they pursue eternally an elusive, ever-shifting banner.

Holding his head in horror, Dante cries out to the spirit that guides him: "Sweet Spirit, what souls are these who run through this black haze?" He is answered: "These are the nearly soulless whose lives concluded neither blame nor praise."[1] The way into hell is filled with those who are nearly soulless, who live only according to their own advantage. We cannot really blame them; but neither can we praise them. The fact is that much of the hellish nature of urban life is a result of the deeds, misdeeds, and nondeeds of the nearly soulless (whether privileged or poor) who live only for themselves, who act only in the interests of self-advantage. And this kind of destructive, crass, self-seeking individualism must be distinguished from the self-interest of congregation-based community organizing.

"Interest" comes from two Latin words: *inter* and *esse*, which literally translate "to be among." Authentic self-interest has to do with the self that is to be among others. The authentic self is discovered in the life that is lived among others, in community, in the public arena. Organizing draws people into community based upon common self-interest. Perhaps we work together to seek drug treatment funding, or to improve public education, or to secure more jobs. Organizing needs to connect with these kinds of short-term self-interest if it hopes to get people involved for whom these issues are real concerns. But organizing also needs to address long-term self-interest: our values, our faith, our need for relationships, our longing for community, our thirst for justice.

In the long run, it is what organizing is about: weaving together a liberative community in which people can live out their values, be connected to a network of significant relationships, and be agitated to summon forth their God-given power and potential. In his book *Denial of Death*, Ernst Becker says that what people fear most is not dying. What people fear most is that when they die, no one will notice. Organizing around self-interest has to do with shaping a life that makes a significant contribution to society, a life that makes a difference, a life that will be missed by others when death comes.

Any discussion of self-interest presumes both a healthy sense of the self and a sense of hope. Self-interest assumes a self that has interests, that has hope, that intends a future for the self, indeed a future built upon that which is of interest to the self. At this point we find that we are already in some difficulty. The difficulty is that all around us we see self-destructive behavior and hopelessness. That difficulty is strikingly set forth for us by Cornel West in his book *Race Matters*.

According to West, nihilism is the most basic issue now facing black America. By nihilism, West means "the lived experience of coping with a life of horrifying meaninglessness, hopelessness, and (most important) lovelessness" resulting in "a numbing detachment from others and a self-destructive disposition toward the world."[2] West sees the nihilistic threat as being generated primarily by market-driven corporate enterprises, the collapse of sustaining cultural structures, and white supremacy.

Perhaps West both overstates and understates his claim. Perhaps it is overstated in that much of black America is still grounded in deeply rooted personal faith. Perhaps it is understated in that nihilism afflicts much more than black America. The suicide of grunge rock star Kurt Cobain is a case in point. What if not nihilism was at the cynical core of Cobain's life and music, which attracted millions of white youth? Consider some of his lyrics—like "Look on the bright side of suicide" or "I'd rather be dead than cool"—from an album that sold ten million copies. Or the title of one of his songs: "I Hate Myself and Want to Die." Similarly, nihilism was at work in the life and suicide death of Rozz Williams, leader of the Gothic Rock band, "Christian Death," whose titles included "Death Wish" and reflected the manic-depressive, alcohol- and drug-abused life of Mr. Williams.

Nihilism, the denial of all existence, a belief in nothingness, is empty of hope and devoid of self-love. Nihilism lacks true awareness of the self and ultimately leads to destruction of the self. The self-destructive tendencies of nihilism are the antithesis of self-interest. Worse yet, nihilism seeks to bring everything to nothingness. Power in the hands of someone whose self is lost to nihilism can only result in destruction. Nihilism uses power to cause nothingness. Our society, our cities, our churches and neighborhoods suffer from the destructive effects of nihilistic power.

I recall going to the Milwaukee County Children's Detention Center to visit a sixteen-year-old youth who had worshiped on several occasions at Incarnation, the congregation I serve. The youth was facing trial as an adult for murdering a woman in front of her ten-year-old daughter in a parking lot. He had a shotgun and intended to rob her. She knelt down and gave him her purse as he had ordered her to do. But she didn't seem frightened. This angered him. He told the police: "I was the man with the gun, but here she was smiling at me. So I shot her." He blew her head away in front of her little daughter. When I visited this young man, I was shaken by his passivity, his almost gentle expression, his lack of remorse, his lack of self-awareness, his apparent inability to grasp why he did what he had done. For me, this young man is a classic example of the nihilism West describes as resulting in a numbing detachment from others and a self-destructive disposition toward the world. And this young man is legion.

We cannot speak in any meaningful way about self-interest without admitting the forcefulness of the nihilistic threat and our need to confront it. We cannot deal with self-interest unless we help to reawaken the self-love, self-respect, and self-awareness that are deadened by nihilism. How can we organize around self-interest when there is self-hate and self-destruction? Our organizing efforts must include what West calls the "politics of conversion," which are grounded not only in power analyses and organizing savvy but in a love ethic. It takes love to create self-love.

The lack of self-love means a lack of self-interest upon which to build a liberated community.

Self-interest has to do with the search for self-love, self-discovery, and community. It is a great journey that, for people of faith, leads to an encounter with God. Biblically, this journey and this encounter are perhaps most dynamically exemplified in the story of Moses and the burning bush. Moses is in exile in the land of Midian, tending to the flock of his father-in-law Jethro, the priest of Midian, at Mt. Horeb. "There the angel of the Lord appeared to him in a flame of fire out of a bush; he looked, and the bush was blazing, yet it was not consumed" (Exod. 3:2). What ensues is a remarkable interaction between God and Moses in which Moses is challenged to be a liberator and God is challenged to reveal God's identity at a new level. As Ernie Cortes says, "the burning bush symbolizes Moses' confrontation with himself."

"The cry of the Israelites has now come to me; I have also seen how the Egyptians oppress them. So come, I will send you to Pharaoh to bring my people, the Israelites, out of Egypt" (Exod. 3:9-10). The initial response of Moses to this awesome command of God is evasive: "Who am I that I should go to Pharaoh, and bring the Israelites out of Egypt?" (Exod. 3:11). This question is not simply a self-deprecating ploy used by Moses to evade God's summons. Here is the son of a Hebrew slave who grew up in the courts of Pharaoh as a prince and is now a fugitive murderer tending sheep in a foreign land. Who indeed is Moses? Slave or prince? Hebrew or Midianite? Murderer or shepherd? Fugitive or liberator? Unless Moses discovers who he really is, what his self-interest truly is, he is of little use to the freedom struggle of the Hebrew slaves. God challenges Moses to see himself the way that God sees him: the bold liberator of the Hebrew people. God's encounter with Moses clarifies Moses' self-interest. Moses now knows who he is.

It is instructive that the struggle of Moses for his identity at the burning bush also issues in the revelation of the divine identity. God reveals to Moses God's name: YHWH, which is commonly translated: "I Am Who I Am." God knows who God is. The divine identity is clear. But who are you, Moses? The struggle for identity, for self-discovery, for knowledge of self-interest, is in its essence a spiritual struggle. The account of Moses at the burning bush suggests to us that as one comes to know oneself, one comes to know God. It is no surprise to those who trust the truth of the creation narratives in Genesis, which teach us that men and women are created in the image of God. Given the *imago Dei*, the discovery of the authentic self means also a discovery of God. We cannot truly discover who we are without also discovering YHWH, the I Am Who I Am, the One who creates us to be the image of God in the world.

Some scholars assert that the holy Tetragrammaton, YHWH, is most accurately translated in the future tense, along the lines of "I Will Be Who I Will Be." In this case the God revealed as YHWH is a God of process, a God continually unfolding, a God eternally becoming. If Moses is called to serve a God who is in the process of becoming, then the question of Moses, "Who am I . . . ?" must be placed alongside another question, "Who will I become?"

Who will I become? The journey toward self-discovery is a journey that never arrives, it is always becoming. Along this journey, identification of self-interest is critical to keeping the movement, the deepening, the growth alive and vital. Clouded or denied self-interest results in stagnation, in limitation, in being stuck. Action in the public arena around self-interest is part of the act of becoming; like a flower in spring, it is a public unfolding of the self.

This process of self-becoming is biblically not a solitary matter between a person and God. Moses will become Moses only through his leadership in the liberation struggles of the Hebrew people. Moses needs the Hebrew tribal community to make possible his own self-becoming. We cannot discover ourselves, we cannot find ourselves, in isolation. The discovery of true self and of true self-interest can only be done in the context of community. Indeed, biblically speaking no "self" is possible apart from the tribe, the community, the nation, the church, or the kingdom.

Congregation-based community organizing encourages the process of self-becoming. And it does so honoring the *imago Dei* present in each person and respecting the precious diversity of self-interests. Each of us is different. That reality has become quite clear to me as the father of two adorable daughters. One Thanksgiving Day, when Nora was seven and Laureena was five, we shared a glorious turkey. After drying the wishbone, I explained the custom to them of making a wish, keeping it secret, and breaking the bone to try for the bigger piece and the fulfillment of the wish. They each made a wish, grabbed an end of the bone, pulled, tugged, and twisted. Nora won. "I'm going to tell you my wish, since it won't come true anyway," said Nora. "It won't come true until the end of the world." "What was your wish?" I asked Nora. "I wished for world peace," she said. "How about you, Laureena?" I asked. "What did you wish for?" She smiled jubilantly and said, "I wished for all the girl toys in the world." I would not wish for Nora to have the self-interest of Laureena or for Laureena to have the self-interest of Nora. In their diversity, I find a great wonder, a great mystery, a great delight. Any lockstep approach to self-interest violates the human soul.

Who am I? Who will I become? Congregation-based community organizing is a process that creates a community of people who share common self-interests and who are deepened in their self-discovery through liberation struggles. The community challenges, encourages, summons forth one's giftedness, fires one's passion. Such a communal journey is akin to that of Moses. Those on such a journey come to realize that they, like Moses, are standing and moving on holy ground.

CHAPTER 7

One-on-Ones

"The next day John again was standing with two of his disciples, and as he watched Jesus walk by, he exclaimed, 'Look, here is the Lamb of God!' The two disciples heard him say this, and they followed Jesus. When Jesus turned and saw them following, he said to them, 'What are you looking for?' They said to him, 'Rabbi, where are you staying?' He said to them, 'Come and see.' They came and saw where he was staying, and they remained with him that day. It was about four o'clock in the afternoon." (John 1:35-39)

The one-on-one interview is the primary tool of organizing. A good organizer continually does one-on-ones and trains leaders to do the same. The one-on-one interview is the building block of an organization. In the initial stages of developing a congregation-based community organization, hundreds of people are trained to conduct thousands of one-on-ones in their churches and neighborhoods. This essential process is repeated every few years in the life of an organization as a means of creating and deepening relationships, staying connected to the self-interests of the grassroots, and expanding the power base of the organization. While shaping an issue and preparing for an action, members of task forces conduct one-on-one interviews with those who have knowledge and influence relative to that issue.

On one level a one-on-one is as natural as a conversation over a backyard fence or with a fellow passenger in an airplane. On another level it is skilled, artful, intentional, and focused. The one-on-one interview is a means of initiating or building a relationship. The primary (and usually only) agenda of a one-on-one is to get to know the other person. It is not a sales pitch. It is not a means of asking another person to do something. It is not an attempt to recruit another person to one's point of view. It is simply a conversation in which we learn another person's self-interest by getting to know him or her. It is a conversation in which we come to understand what is important to another person, what motivates him or her, what is his or her passion. We can only come to understand as we learn something about his or her childhood, family, job, education, faith, church, politics, hobbies, disappointments, dreams, anger, ambition.

A leader or organizer conducting a one-on-one interview must bring curiosity and courage to the conversation. An organizer must hold genuine interest in the story being told and in the life journey of the other person. If the one being interviewed senses boredom or judgment, he or she will keep the conversation superficial and will not reveal much of significance. Without being intrusive, the interviewer needs to take the risk of probing to discover the motivational depths of the other person. It means listening for areas of tragedy, pain, anger, passion, and injustice in the other person's life story.

A successful one-on-one interview, in the space of about a half-hour, initiates or deepens a relationship, uncovers the other person's self-interest, allows the other person to gain clarity about what motivates him or her, and acquires essential knowledge about the person. The one-on-one interview is a simple, relational tool. A healthy and vital congregation-based community organization cannot be built without it.

Organizing is essentially a relational process. At its best organizing is rooted in unconditional love for other persons, which seeks relationships that move toward empowerment, community, and justice. At its heart, organizing is about relationships, not issues. Organizing misses its calling when it becomes a swirl of frenetic activity, addicted to issues and actions, running past and over human beings. One-on-ones slow things down, restore needed focus, serve as a reminder of the human dimension of this work.

As Mick Roschke, a stellar Milwaukee pastor said, "Every person is a treasure. That's why we do one-on-ones." One-on-ones honor the image of God within another person. The expectation is that a great discovery is to be made in seeking to know any human being. Such an expectation stands in contradiction to counseling sessions that focus on the guilt, failure, and neuroses of another person or to social work approaches that concentrate on the needs and limitations of another person. One-on-ones do not allow a spirit of condescension. On the contrary, the interviewer comes as supplicant, seeking to learn, to know, to discover. Franz Kafka wrote: "Life's splendor forever lies in wait about each one of us in all its fullness, but veiled from view, deep down, invisible, far off. It is there, though, not hostile, not reluctant, not deaf. If you summon it by the right word, by its right name, it will come." The one-on-one interview is the right word, the right name for releasing life's splendor dwelling within the life stories of those around us.

The conversations of Jesus, as recorded in the Gospels, are never casual. He confronts, challenges, invites, admonishes. His words are "sharper than any two edged-sword, piercing until dividing soul from spirit." In all conversation with Jesus a deepening occurs. Relationship is sought, but it is always rooted in truth. Those who cannot handle the truth walk away from him.

As cited at the beginning of this chapter, the first words out of the mouth of Jesus in the Gospel of John are "What are you looking for?" The first command of Jesus recorded by John is "Come and see." The first action of Jesus in John's Gospel is to spend a late afternoon and evening establishing a relationship with two disciples of John the Baptist. These examples are instructive as we look at one-on-ones through the lens of faith.

"What are you looking for?" The Greek word used here in the Gospel of John, *zatein*, has a double meaning. It is a word that can operate on two levels. And so the question of Jesus to the two disciples of John the Baptist could have the sense of either "What do you want?" or "What are you searching for?" The distinction is between superficiality and depth. Do the disciples simply want to satisfy their curiosity? Do they simply want to find out a few things about Jesus? Or are they searching for meaning, for the Messiah, for salvation?

"What do you want?" The question needs to be turned on the one-on-one interviewer. What do I want out of this one-on-one? Am I truly interested in this person, in his or her life story, in establishing a relationship? Or am I engaging in this conversation only to find out a few things about him or her, only to gather some useful data so that I can report back to the organization? Perhaps I am only feigning interest in this conversation. I want the person to imagine that I am interested in her or him so that I can get her or him back into active membership in my congregation or signed up for a task force of my organization.

If I want this kind of thing out of my one-on-ones, then I am objectifying the people I am interviewing. I do not really want *the person*. I want only what that person can offer me. The superficiality and utilitarian nature of my interest will be transparent and duly noted by the person interviewed. No relationship will be established. The truth will remain concealed.

"What are you searching for?" Here is the question that Jesus hopes will engage the two disciples. He is looking for searchers, for seekers, for those who probe the depths of life. The early church was called The Way. It was not called The Answer or The Destination. Those who follow Jesus are searchers on a Way that never arrives in this life.

"What are you searching for?" When the one-on-one interview engages at this level, a relationship is formed. A discovery is made. The jewel of a person's life story is mined and polished. The person being interviewed senses that we are actually interested in them. We are not there to take from them but to listen and to draw forth. One searcher is listening to another. A sacred conversation occurs in which the image of God in one person listens to the image of God in the other.

A street alcoholic named Jesse had been coming to our emergency food pantry on and off for a couple of years. I found him to be obnoxious and annoying. I saw nothing good in him but had never bothered to take the time to get to know him. One day I decided to do a one-on-one with him. I learned that Jesse Lipman has spent twenty-two of his fifty-four years of life in prison. He lost his Social Security Insurance (SSI) a year ago when alcoholism was no longer viewed as a disease meriting SSI benefits. Without income or any residence for more than a year, Jesse has somehow managed to survive. He likes to play chess. He likes to play the tenor sax if he can get his hands on one. While in prison, he learned woodworking and drafting, completed his GED, and took some college courses. Now and then he feels tempted to assault someone in order to get some money. So far he has resisted these temptations. Having done a one-on-one interview with Jesse, I can no longer write him off as just another street alcoholic. He is an intelligent, complex person with a range of gifts who has both inflicted and endured suffering. He is, like me, a child of God.

Through this one-on-one interviewing process, I have developed a profound respect for members of the congregation that I serve in Milwaukee. I sense the strength, faith, and willpower of those who grew up down South as the children of sharecroppers, some deprived of education because they worked in cotton fields at the age of eight, all facing the brutality of racial hatred and Jim Crow laws. I admire the courage of one woman who did a solitary sit-in at a segregated department store when she was in high school. I grieve for another whose husband was murdered by two white men whose punishment was a weekend in jail. I marvel at another who was raised in poverty, started out as a school secretary, and ended up with a Ph.D. from Columbia University and a principal in the Milwaukee Public School system. The stories of struggle, of the primacy of the church community and faith in Jesus, of dreams and aspirations for oneself and one's family, of the pain of losing one's children to the streets, of achievements in education and the workplace—all such stories and more reveal the dignity, pain, and wonder of personhood. To hear such stories is an honor. To hear such stories is to hear the heartbeat of the soul.

The first words of Jesus in the Gospel of John, "What are you looking for?" yield to another question in chapter 20 when the resurrected Jesus asks Mary Magdalene outside of the tomb, "Whom are you looking for?" The "What are you looking for?" at the beginning of Jesus' ministry leads to the "Whom are you looking for?" after his resurrection. The search of our lives for meaning, purpose, and hope cannot be satisfied in a What, even if that What is as sacred as a doctrine or a church. Such searching seeks a Whom. It is the person of Jesus who saves us, not a theology about Jesus. It is the persons in a congregation who form Christian community, not the institution of a church.

And so also the one-on-one interview looks not so much for the What as for the Whom. We are not looking so much for information *about* a person as we are looking *for* the person. In my interview with Jesse, I needed to look for the person of Jesse and beyond the What of a street alcoholic. Using the language of Martin Buber, at that moment we move from an I-It to an I-Thou relationship.[1]

The first command of Jesus recorded in the Gospel of John is "Come and see." These words of Jesus to the two disciples of John the Baptist are both an invitation and an imperative. It is a critical moment in the course of their lives. If they do not come and see, they will miss out on the most important relationship of their lives. It is not enough to claim that they are searching for something or someone. It is necessary that they commit to that claim through an intentional encounter with Jesus. Likewise, it is not enough for us to claim that we are interested in building Christian community. We need to come and see the stories, the dwelling places of others. We need to be intentional about entering into the lives of others.

Teilhard de Chardin said: "God only enters when you reach for the other." It is a religious act to reach for the other, to break the isolation and individualism of this diseased culture. God may be found within me, but this discovery is best made by others. It is spiritually hazardous for most of us to imagine that we can encounter God apart from community. When

I look within for God, I am most likely to see my own projections, my own imaginings, my own myopic notions about God. Or else I will despair because I see only my failings, depravity, and sin.

When I reach for the other, seeking the soul of another, seeking the image of God within the other, I am more likely to encounter an authentic spiritual experience. In coming to know others, I come to know God in new ways. The promise of Jesus is to be present when two or three are gathered together in the Lord's name. Such intentionality of Christian relationship widens the soul to receive the presence of Jesus.

We need to be intentional and vigilant in building relationships. As attentive as the monk who guards what he believes to be the Ark of the Covenant in Ethiopia. Many Ethiopians are convinced that the Ark of the Covenant has lain in Aksum, Ethiopia's most sacred city, for nearly 3,000 years. Kept within a solid gold case inside a square stone temple next to the ancient St. Mary of Zion Church is a white stone tablet with the Ten Commandments inscribed, according to Coptic Ethiopians, by the very hand of God. This Ark is guarded by a solitary monk. At midnight each night, this guardian monk begins burning incense and praying incessantly, reading the Psalms and other Scripture. He keeps vigil over the Ark until 3 P.M. the next day, when he is allowed to rest and eat. Thus, each day the monk conducts an unbroken, fifteen-hour vigil over the Ark. Such attentiveness and vigilance are incomprehensible to our society of continual distractions, frenetic energy, and capacity to observe little more than sound bites.

Given the belief of the Ethiopians, their Ark in Aksum merits sacred vigilance. But what about the human heart, upon which God promises (according to Jeremiah 31) to write His/Her law and which is (according to 1 Cor. 6) a temple of the Holy Spirit? Is not the human heart also a holy Ark that merits sacred vigilance? One-on-one interviews are a heart-to-heart conversation. Would that we could bring even a portion of the vigilance of that Ethiopian guardian monk to such conversations. We might then begin to see the presence of God in the other.

CHAPTER 8

Agitation

"When they had finished breakfast, Jesus said to Simon Peter, 'Simon son of John, do you love me more than these?' He said to him, 'Yes, Lord; you know that I love you.' Jesus said to him, 'Feed my lambs.' A second time he said to him, 'Simon son of John, do you love me?' He said to him, 'Yes, Lord; you know that I love you.' Jesus said to him, 'Tend my sheep.' He said to him the third time, 'Simon son of John, do you love me?' Peter felt hurt because he said to him the third time, 'Do you love me?' And he said to him, 'Lord, you know everything; you know that I love you.' Jesus said to him, 'Feed my sheep.'" (John 21:15-17)

I am a somewhat introverted, shy person. So, when the session on "Agitation" began to heat up at the national weeklong training of the Gamaliel Foundation, I wondered how I could have been stupid enough to sit in the front row. Usually I am a master of concealment. Now I felt uncomfortably exposed. Greg Galluzzo, executive director of Gamaliel and trainer for this session, was hovering over me, his voice rising more than a few decibels. "I've known you for two years, and I still don't get your self-interest! You're all mushy and fuzzy. I don't know whether you want to be an iconographer or a parish pastor." "You've been on my case all morning, Greg," I protested. "What do you want from me? I've already gotten $50,000 from the Lutheran Church for MICAH." (This effort at deflection and vaunting of achievement was a serious mistake. It only got Greg angrier and deepened the spotlight on me.) "What do I want from you? $50,000 is peanuts! I want you to get $50 million, $75 million from the banks for the inner city of Milwaukee. . . . Look, if you want to leave the parish ministry and MICAH and go off somewhere and paint icons, do it. There's nothing wrong in that. That would be beautiful. Just make up your mind."

Years later I still have vivid recollection of that interaction. Greg cared enough for me, saw enough within me, believed enough in me to agitate me to move forward with more clarity in my life. Such agitation, as uncomfortable and confrontational as it may be, is an act of love.

Agitation is a skill. For organizers it is a vehicle for summoning forth the best from their leaders.

Agitation is a means of getting others to act out of their own power and self-interest, out of their own vision for their life. Agitation is not a way of getting someone to do what I want them to do. Greg was clear about what he wanted from me in terms of inner-city banking practices, but what he really wanted was for me to discern my self-interest, my vision for my life, and for me to act on the basis of such discernment.

Relationship is a prerequisite of agitation. I have no right to agitate people I do not know. If I don't know what their self-interests are, who they are, what potentiality they have, I am in no position to agitate them to live out their vision for their lives. Properly speaking, there is no such thing as an "outside agitator." An agitator is trying to create community, build an organization, raise up leaders. An agitator is relationally connected to the one being agitated.

Most churches do not operate on the basis of healthy agitation that is rooted in relationship and that summons forth the best from their people. They operate instead on the basis of manipulation, authoritarianism, or guilt-tripping. A pastor may feign special interest in someone as a means of getting her or him to accept a position in the church. The not-too-subtle suggestion may be given that if this person were *really* a Christian then of course he or she would be glad to serve on this or that committee. If Jesus died for you, the least you can do is serve as stewardship chairperson. In some churches, the authority of the pastor is such that he or she can more or less order a person to do what is needed. But guilt-tripping remains a favorite. Everyone else has been giving their all around here; can't you? The church has always been there for you; now it's time for you to be there for the church. We're really depending on you. If you don't lead the evangelism committee, I'm afraid that the future doesn't look too promising for our church.

In contrast we note the interaction between Jesus and Simon Peter in John 21. Jesus is direct and honest. "Simon son of John, do you love me more than these?" Simon is stripped of the name Cephas or Peter which had been given to him by Jesus in John 1. His threefold denial of Jesus in the courtyard of the high priest (John 18), despite his bravado that he would lay down his life for Jesus (John 13), is humiliating evidence that he is not worthy for now of being called Peter, the Rock. "Simon son of John, do you love me?" Three times Simon denied Jesus. Three times he is summoned to declare his love.

The agitation of Simon Peter by Jesus is rooted in relationship. Jesus loves Simon and sees in him the leader of the early Church. He also foresees the martyrdom of Peter. He will indeed lay down his life for Jesus. "But when you grow old, you will stretch out your hands, and someone else will fasten a belt around you and take you where you do not wish to go."

If Simon Peter loves Jesus, as he so adamantly claims, then his potentiality must be summoned forth. Jesus agitates him. "Feed my lambs." "Tend my sheep." "Feed my sheep." As long as Simon is crippled by his fear and by his remorse, he is immobilized and useless as a leader. By summoning forth Simon's declaration of love for Jesus and by entrusting Simon with the feeding and tending of Jesus' Church, Jesus heals Simon. He restores Simon to his vision of himself, one who is like a rock in his love for Jesus and in his willingness to serve, to lead, and to lay down his life for his Lord.

Another example of the agitational style of Jesus is seen in John 5. A man who is an invalid among invalids at the pool of Beth-zatha (or Bethesda) by the Sheep Gate in Jerusalem has been ill for thirty-eight years and lies amidst the blind, the lame, and the paralyzed. "When Jesus saw him lying there and knew that he had been there for a long time, he said to him, 'Do you want to be made well?'" What kind of question is that? What would it be like to be on the receiving end of such a question? It sounds heartless and callous, a blaming of the victim. Knowing that the man had been lying there as an invalid for a long time, how could Jesus ask such a question?

Jesus makes no assumption that the man wants to be healed. Perhaps the man is comfortable with being an invalid. As a parish pastor, I encounter people now and then who do not really want to be healed. They would never, of course, openly admit to it, but the truth is that their identity has become wrapped up in their illness. It is how they get attention. It is how they withdraw from a demanding world. It is how they get cared for. It is how they can feed their self-pity. It is how they can give up on life without incurring any blame.

The man who has been ill for thirty-eight years is at a crossroads. Jesus is agitating him. His answer is evasive. "Sir, I have no one to put me into the pool when the water is stirred up; and while I am making my way, someone else steps down ahead of me." We would have preferred a bolder response. The man offers excuses. When an angel stirs the water and gives it healing power, someone else always gets into the pool first. It is the language of the perpetual victim. Everyone else has the breaks. Fate has dealt me a rotten hand. Those less deserving than I have greater success.

Jesus refuses to see the man as a victim. He refuses to acknowledge the man's excuses. Most pastors or laity at this point would offer their commiseration, their sympathy, their prayers. Not Jesus. He sees within the man something else, a potentiality that has lain dormant for so many years, a possibility that the man himself has trouble seeing. The agitation of Jesus becomes direct and confrontational. He now forces the man to make a decision. "Stand up, take your mat and walk." Amazingly, the man is healed. He casts aside his victim role, his supine posture, his invalid identity. He takes up his mat and begins to walk.

Why take the mat? What does the mat have to do with the man's healing? Jesus wants the man to take his history with him, to take with him a visual, tangible reminder of what he lived through. He is not to forget, when he encounters other invalids, what it means to be an invalid: the dependency, the humiliation, the despair, and the seduction of viewing oneself as victim. The agitation of Jesus releases the man's potentiality, shapes his healing, and prepares him to be a wounded healer of others.

Agitation is a summoning forth of one's vision for one's life in defiance of all those cultural forces that press down upon a person so that by middle age a restless settling in takes place, an accommodation to meaningless work, unsatisfying relationships, and an unjust society. Such is the fate of J. Alfred Prufrock in T. S. Eliot's poem, "The Love Song of J. Alfred Prufrock." As he ages, his dreams reflect his mediocrity: "I grow old . . . I grow old . . . / I shall wear the bottoms of my trousers rolled. / . . . Do I dare to eat a peach?" Without someone to agitate us, even people of faith succumb to the malaise of society and to an inertia of the soul. Tragedy permeates the air when a person abandons the great questions to settle for the banal.

In 1946 while riding on a train in suburban Calcutta, Mother Teresa experienced what she described as her "divine call within a call." She was doing good work as a suburban school administrator. But now Mother Teresa was called "to live among the poor and there to serve God." Her obedience to this call relieved the suffering of thousands of people dying on streets, brought mercy to even more people languishing in abject poverty, and touched the consciences of millions. The world was made a little more human because Mother Teresa listened to the voice of God.

At its best, agitation touches on the matter of vocation. A "divine call within a call" is issued for each person, whether we hear or heed it or not. That fact that I have been called to be a baptized Christian does not resolve the matter of my call within a call. Where is my life leading?

What is the purpose of my life? What are God's dreams for me? Agitation claims that more is yet to come to my life, to my potentiality, to my divine call within a call. Agitation confronts, urges, probes, explores the question of vocation.

The story is told of a medical doctor who parachuted into a foreign land. Equipped with valuable medicines, she intended to land in a remote village. Instead, the wind caused her parachute to drift. She landed in a tree, got caught in its branches, and hung suspended about twenty feet above the ground. After an hour or so, she noticed a man walking by. "Excuse me," she called out. "How do I get into town?" "Just take this road straight into the village," said the man, who proceeded to walk past her on his way. Noticing that the man was wearing a clerical collar, the medical doctor cried out, "And what do you do for a living?" Turning around the pastor said, "I, Ma'am, am a man of God!" "I should have known," shouted the doctor. "You speak the truth, but you don't do me a darn bit of good."

Agitation does not leave people hanging. It honors the valuable gifts that they bring. It summons them to release those gifts in service of their vision for their lives. And it connects them to a community, such as a church or a congregation-based community organization, where their gifts can be actualized and their leadership developed.

Agitation is impolite. It is direct and confrontational, and it creates tension. Agitation is a difficult skill to be learned by people who have been brought up to think that niceness is the *sine qua non* of saintliness. It is also a difficult skill to be learned by those who enjoy running over other people. A balancing act is required here. As Che Guevara said: "One must be hard, but without losing tenderness."

The most profound experiences of my life were being present for the births of my two daughters. My memory is vivid. Nora, because of her breech presentation during birth, was manually rotated in Lynn's womb by a nurse. Laureena's heart rate dropped in half with each contraction because the umbilical cord was wrapped around her throat. For Lynn the ecstasy of birthing overcame the severe pain and exhaustion of contractions, transition, and delivery. It meant blood, struggle, intensity, and risk—the cost of giving life.

Agitation also seeks to summon forth life. It cannot do so without struggle, tension, and risk. It may be painful for both the agitator and the person being agitated, but pain is the worthwhile cost of giving birth to new life.

CHAPTER 9

Metropolitan Organizing

"And see, I am sending upon you what my Father promised; so stay here in the city until you have been clothed with power from on high." (Luke 24:49)

Thirty years ago Gary, Indiana, had a thriving downtown business district with a newly constructed convention center. Its steel mills employed thousands of workers. It had elected the first African American mayor of any major city in the United States. Gary was a city with poverty, to be sure. But Gary was also a city with promise. Today, Gary is overwhelmed with abandoned homes; its business district is essentially abandoned; it has lost tens of thousands of jobs; it is the murder capitol of the nation.[1]

The metropolitan region of Gary, on the other hand, is thriving. Thousands of new homes have been built, huge shopping malls and commercial developments have been constructed, and tens of thousands of jobs have been created. An economic and racial apartheid is at work. The city of Gary suffers a collapsed economy while the suburban region sees its economy growing. The urban poor of Gary are primarily people of color. The financially privileged suburbanites are primarily white.

Gary is not alone in its experience of metropolitan disparity. An urban underclass exists alongside of suburban prosperity in cities across the United States. The economic disparity generally plays out along racial lines. The conditions would be considered intolerable in any moral society. Family-sustaining jobs have vanished in the neighborhoods of the underclass. Drug trafficking constitutes a main part of the underclass economy. Schools are in near meltdown mode. The housing stock has lost its value. Prisons have become the institution of higher learning for a disturbing percentage of underclass youth. Hopelessness, fear, ill health, survival behavior, dependency, and a continual state of crisis are prevalent.

Cities have always struggled with poverty, but their economic and political clout kept them from being overwhelmed by it. Increasingly, capital and political strength are moving to the suburbs as cities shrink and weaken. The City of St. Louis has declined from more than 600,000 people to just about 300,000. Buffalo and Cleveland show similar statistical decline. The city of Detroit used to have a population of two million people. Now, amidst tracts of vacant lots and abandoned buildings live fewer than one million.

Urban sprawl weakens the tax base of America's troubled cities and deepens racial and class division. It drains limited tax dollars for highway construction and infrastructure for new housing developments, turns farmland into subdivisions, wreaks environmental havoc, and erects endless shopping malls. It moves jobs and industry further and further away from the urban underclass. The damage inflicted on our cities by urban sprawl is lasting and considerable.

Over and against the destruction caused by urban sprawl, David Rusk argues for a policy of regionalization of planning, taxing, and spending.[2] He points to Indianapolis as a positive example of regionalization. When now Senator Richard Lugar was mayor of Indianapolis, he finessed a state legislative action that made the boundaries of Indianapolis and its surrounding county congruent, creating a "uni-government." The effects have been dramatic. Rusk contrasts Indianapolis, an "elastic" city, with Milwaukee, an "inelastic" city hemmed in by surrounding suburbs. Although both cities have similar total populations and similar numbers of poor and minorities, Indianapolis spreads out its city services more equitably and does not suffer from the severe ghettoization of the poor that exists in Milwaukee. Rusk points to regionalization in Portland, Oregon, as another success story.

Myron Orfield similarly points to the devastation caused by urban sprawl that leaves in its wake an increasing number of census tracts of concentrated poverty in America's cities.[3] Like Rusk, Orfield advocates for a policy of regionalization. To counter the ghettoization of poverty, Orfield proposes regional strategies such as tax-based revenue sharing, fair distribution of low-income housing, convergence of school districts, and equitable spread of transportation dollars to create access to jobs.

Orfield's studies show that it is not only the urban core that suffers from the current fractionalization; the inner ring suburbs also suffer and begin to show the same signs of decay as inner cities while prosperity continues its outward flight. Orfield's analysis of the Chicago area shows that more than two-thirds of the metropolitan population would benefit from a policy of regionalization. Many older, inner-ring suburbs are comprised of blue-collar, working class populations that actually have much in common with the self-interests of those trapped in the urban core when it comes to the impact of urban sprawl.

An increasing number of urban planners, politicians, and business leaders are beginning to see the wisdom in regionalization. But entrenched opposition is also present. Most politicians in dying, urban communities are secure in their local power base and rightly understand that their political future could be at risk in an expanded electorate. Developers of new subdivisions are making their fortunes through urban sprawl. Construction industries and union laborers benefit from the building of highways and shopping malls. Racism and fear of the urban poor continue to fuel the outward migration from America's cities.

A metropolitan approach to organizing offers the primary hope of countering such opposition to regionalization. Powerful metropolitan organizations that join the self-interests of inner-ring suburbs and urban cores can force the implementation of regional strategies and solutions to the problems of urban America. It is a daunting task. Community organizations also have their comfort zones and sense of turf. Like politicians, leaders in community organizations may fear that their role will be diminished if the organization goes metropolitan. Many would prefer to be a big fish in a small pond to becoming one of many big fish in a large lake. Racial mistrust and class division afflict community organizations like every other institution. A fixation on the crises of daily existence in the urban core prevents many leaders from stepping back to see the larger picture, to do effective analysis, to imagine substantive solutions. Many of those in the inner-ring suburbs prefer to dwell in a state of denial, persisting in the illusion that they have escaped the woes of the urban core. Congregation-based community organizing needs to draw on Scripture and faith as a means of creating the vision and moral mandate needed to overcome the many obstacles to metropolitan organizing.

Let us reflect first for a bit on vision. As an evangelistic religion, Christianity has always had a vision for expansion. Historically, the church has taken seriously the Great Commission of Jesus to "make disciples of all nations." All too often this activity was done through the outrageous option of death or baptism, or through an unholy alliance with imperialistic interests, or through a total disregard for indigenous cultures. But it was done. And the church today, even as it acknowledges the sin that stains its often-heroic missionary history, still evangelizes without regard to boundaries. The church claims the world for its Lord.

Congregation-based community organizing, which offers a rare fidelity to the justice dimension of faith, must also draw on the evangelistic fervor of the missionary dimension of faith. The disciples were told by Jesus to stay in the city until they were clothed with power from on high. Congregation-based community organizations, having been clothed with such power, must consider whether they have stayed within the narrow confines of the city too long. A metropolitan power base is needed to bring about policies of regionalization. Without such policies, the conditions of the urban core and inner-ring suburbs will only worsen. Congregation-based community organizing must develop the same sweeping vision for justice that the church has for evangelism. No boundaries. Continual expansion of the power base.

The outpouring of the Holy Spirit on Pentecost propelled the early church beyond the city of Jerusalem with a fervor that changed the course of history. The Pentecostal gift of tongues enabled the disciples to proclaim the gospel to Jews gathered in Jerusalem "from every nation under heaven" in the native languages of the Judeans, the Parthians, the Medes, the Elamites, the Mesopotamians, the Cappadocians, the Phrygians, the Pamphylians, the Egyptians, the Libyans, and the Romans. Neither language nor national origin was to block the advance of the gospel. And the gospel was to honor the integrity of both language and national origin. So also, metropolitan organizing will succeed only as people of faith in the suburbs and in the city speak each other's "language" and respect each other's "origin." An honesty must be present about the racial and cultural barriers that exist in order for trust in the power of the Spirit to help people overcome those barriers.

The great hero of the early missionary efforts, St. Paul, had to combat racism and legalism within the church in his efforts to claim the world for the gospel of Jesus. The "dividing wall of hostility" that separated Jew and Gentile had to be broken down. Circumcision and other legal requirements of Jewish tradition had to be declared null and void for Christians. Efforts to force Gentiles to become like Jews would only serve as an impediment to the gospel. Paul had to learn to become "all things to all people" in his desire to spread the gospel among various cultures. In doing so, he offered a model of respect for cultural diversity that is badly needed today.

As congregation-based community organizing goes metropolitan, it confronts the "dividing wall of hostility" between races and classes in this society. No room is available in metropolitan organizing for racial separatism or racial condescension. There is no room for the well-educated to feel superior to the under-educated. There is no room for the privileged to patronize or disdain the underclass. And there is no room for the poor to wallow in victimization and self-deprecation. Metropolitan organizing offers the gracious opportunity for racially and class-based prejudicial suspicions and biased assumptions to be exposed to the light of honest relationships. As people of various colors, cultures, and classes discover their common self-interests, encounter the commonality of their religious belief, and struggle alongside each other in pursuit of common goals, divisions of race and class are transcended by the community of faith.

Much promise lies in metropolitan organizing: the promise of transcending the barriers of race and class, the promise of creating equitable solutions to regional injustices, the promise of weaving metropolitan organizations into national networks with a national justice agenda. The external barriers to realizing such promise are real and considerable. But the primary barriers may be internal. The barriers and the promise bring to mind the story of the twelve spies and the land of Canaan.

Like the twelve spies, those envisioning metropolitan organizing are scouting out a new territory and considering whether this new territory is really capable of being won. In the case of the twelve spies, ten failed in their mission of scouting out the promised land. They saw for themselves that Canaan was a land flowing with milk and honey. They carried back on their shoulders some fruit of the land. But they were afraid. The opposition seemed too formidable. It was not simply that they saw, as part of their proper assessment as spies, the strength of the enemy, the great obstacles that they had to overcome to take the land. The problem was that they mythologized the opposition and denigrated themselves. "There we saw the Nephilim; and to ourselves we seemed like grasshoppers, and so we seemed to them" (Num. 13:33).

At first the spies had reported seeing the descendants of Anak in Canaan (Num. 13:28). Now they call the Anakites the Nephilim, the mythological giants who were the offspring when the sons of God went into the daughters of humans as recorded in Genesis 6. Human enemies were now perceived to be mythological giants. And the ten spies cried out, "To ourselves we seemed like grasshoppers, and so we seemed to them." The spies wilted before the enemy, lost all sense of their own power and potential as God's people, felt like little grasshoppers. They gave over their power to the enemy and empowered the enemy to see them as they saw themselves—as weak as grasshoppers.

Clearly, this danger is always present, this trap of mythologizing the opposition and the obstacles that stand between us and what God has promised us. This propensity is strong to want to give up because of the immensity of the task at hand and the barriers that stand between us and our dreams. We see only giants. Also, this temptation to diminish ourselves creeps in to claim our weakness rather than our power. And it has the advantage of giving us an easy out from God's claims on us. After all, how can grasshoppers be expected to contend with giants?

Metropolitan organizing requires that we see reality. The opposition and the obstacles must be seen for what they are. Perhaps a congregation-based community organization is not yet strong enough to go metropolitan. Perhaps it is. Perhaps the opposition to metropolitan organizing in a given area is simply too formidable. Perhaps it is not. One thing is clear. In this discernment process the people of God must not mythologize the opposition as the Nephilim or denigrate themselves as grasshoppers. Let us see the world as it is.

Caleb is not like the other spies. He sees the opposition in Canaan for what it is. He sees the strength of the Anakites. But he wants to get up at once and take the land. He trusts that the power of God, which delivered the Hebrew people from slavery, will also give them the strength to occupy the promised land.

Caleb is forty years old at this point. Later, in Joshua 15, we hear of Caleb again. He is now eighty-five years old—forty years of desert wanderings plus another five years of warfare in Canaan. Now it is time for distribution of the promised land that should have been entered so many years ago. Joshua honors the promises of Moses and lets Caleb choose whatever portion of land he wants. And what does he choose? He requests of Joshua the hill country of Hebron because the Anakites are there in great, fortified cities. He says to Joshua, "Here I am today, eighty-five years old. I am still as strong today as I was on the day that Moses sent me; my strength now is as my strength was then." With God's help Caleb determines to drive out the Anakites. After all these years he proves at last that they are not the Nephilim after all. They are only Anakites. And he is Caleb with God at his side. Caleb drives them out and takes the land.

Even though my nonviolent spirit chills at these militaristic ventures, and the images of conquest do not fit the vision of metropolitan organizing, this point remains: Caleb is inspiring. He is courageous, undaunted, and determined, and he has a strength that is unlimited by age. Such leaders are needed in the considerable task of metropolitan organizing: people who are not afraid to fight against enormous obstacles in the struggle for justice; people whose faith in the promises of God gives them faith in themselves and in the community that struggles with them; and people whose belief that they can win makes it likely that they will win.

The Calebs are to be discovered both in the churches of the inner city and in the churches of the suburbs. It may be difficult for urban Christians to accept. As an inner-city pastor, I know the insidious inclination to feel self-righteous and morally superior to the suburban Christian. I am painfully aware of the proclivity to view the church of the poor as the "true" church. I know the tendency to guilt-trip suburbanites or to make them feel as though they are the enemy. All of these dispositions, of course, are a sinful violation of the activity of the Holy Spirit who calls, gathers, enlightens, and sanctifies the whole Christian church on earth regardless of racial, class, or geographical boundaries. The Holy Spirit is no respecter of zip codes. Neither should we be.

"I believe in the holy catholic Church." This ancient credal confession, dating as early as the second century, compels the visible church to seek healing of its divisions and to reflect more fully the unity of the invisible church. This confession of faith sounds hollow and false when urban and suburban Christians make the credal proclamation with their lips but do nothing with their hands to bridge the racial and class divisions that separate them. The observation of Dr. Martin Luther King, Jr., that eleven o'clock on a Sunday morning is the most segregated hour of the week still holds true today. Metropolitan organizing provides an opportunity for the church to be true to its calling to be the church catholic, the church universal. Suburban and urban Christians engaged in metropolitan organizing will learn that their shared faith and their shared self-interests transcend the barriers that have divided them.

The question of self-interest is a special challenge to suburban Christians when it comes to metropolitan organizing. The challenge is minimal for those Christians, primarily blue collar, who reside in aging, first ring suburbs. After all, the analysis of Myron Orfield consistently points to the socioeconomic benefits that regionalization can offer such communities. They have much in common with the urban core. The self-interest here is clear. But what about Christians residing in prosperous suburbs and in the affluent communities newly created by urban sprawl?

Regionalization may in fact mean a tax-based revenue sharing that is not in their favor; it may mean the construction of low-income housing in their neighborhood. It may also mean that their children will be educated in a school system that is a consolidation of urban and suburban school districts, and that transportation dollars will be spent on buses to get central city workers to suburban jobs instead of on new highways. Depending on their view, regionalization may be seen as directly counter to their self-interest.

For such prosperous Christians, a hard question surfaces. Does the self-interest of faithfulness to the gospel and to the church catholic transcend socioeconomic self-interest? Are such Christians willing to divest some of their power and some of their privilege for the sake of the larger community, for the sake of their faith, for the sake of the church? Can such Christians escape the heretical snare of the prosperity gospel and remain loyal to the Lord Jesus who "though he was rich for our sakes became poor"? Is the self-interest of values more compelling than the self-interest of money?

Biblically, the hopeful image here is that of Zacchaeus. It is interesting that he is named. In the parable of the rich man and Lazarus, the rich man is not honored with a name. The rich young ruler who turns away from Jesus rather than give away his possessions is not honored with a name. But Zacchaeus is named, although it is also noted that he is short in stature. Jesus, who is so at home with the poor, also seeks out the rich. He invites himself to Zacchaeus's home for dinner. Zacchaeus is delighted. But we are told that "All who saw it began to grumble and said, 'He has gone to be the guest of one who is a sinner'"(Luke 19:7). Here we hear the voice of those Christians who condemn their rich brothers and sisters and who would exclude them from the all-inclusive community of the church.

But Zacchaeus is not put off. He is in fact converted. "Look, half of my possessions, Lord, I will give to the poor; and if I have defrauded anyone of anything, I will pay back four times as much." What is in it for Zacchaeus? Where is his self-interest in such a generous offer? It seems that his only interest at this point is to be in the continuing presence of the Guest who has welcomed him. "Then Jesus said to him, 'Today salvation has come to this house, because he too is a son of Abraham.'" He too is a son of Abraham. The rich too are the children of God. They too have the right to be welcomed to the table of metropolitan organizing. And if they come, if they see in the faces of the urban poor their own brothers and sisters, and if they are willing to divest some of their power and some of their privilege, then the proclamation of Jesus applies also to them: Today salvation has come to this house.

Metropolitan organizing is not about class warfare. In fact the opposite is the case. Metropolitan organizing offers a chance to end the warfare against the poor and to heal the divisions of class and race that separate this sick society. Metropolitan organizing provides a table wide enough to offer a place for all, including the rich, whose compelling self-interest may be their desire to restore their humanity, to live out their faith, to obey their Lord, to honor the church catholic. Some things must be done simply because they are right.

CHAPTER 10

Building and Sustaining an Organization

"But speaking the truth in love, we must grow up in every way into him who is the head, into Christ, from whom the whole body, joined and knit together by every ligament with which it is equipped, as each part is working properly, promotes the body's growth in building itself up in love." (Eph. 4:15-16)

Nelson Mandela, in his autobiography *Long Walk to Freedom*, writes: "The freedom struggle [is] not merely a question of making speeches, holding meetings, passing resolutions, and sending deputations, but of meticulous organization, militant mass action, and, above all, the willingness to suffer and sacrifice."[1] Meticulous organization. Militant mass action. The willingness to suffer and sacrifice. This triadic formula of Nelson Mandela for the freedom struggle is tough stuff. Meticulous organization requires ongoing discipline. Militant mass action is fueled by righteous anger. The willingness to suffer and sacrifice demands enduring courage. The long walk to freedom is, in the words of Jesus, a "narrow path" that few are prepared to take.

The struggle for a truly free and just society goes nowhere if its leaders are primarily interested in making speeches, conducting meetings, and carving out a comfortable place for their ego expansion. The struggle dies on the vine if it is built around a few charismatic individuals without constructing powerful organizations with trained leadership, an expanding network of relationships, and a solid financial base. To speak of the "freedom struggle," "a just society," and "metropolitan equities" is only to use empty rhetoric if we are content with moderate, cathartic adjustments to entrenched, oppressive systems. If the pain and human degradation all around us doesn't stir up within us sufficient anger to want to shake the foundations of this society, then it's probably best for us to go back to playing church and to leave organizing to those whose commitment is real.

"Above all, the willingness to suffer and sacrifice"—this part of Mandela's triadic formula for freedom should come as no surprise to Christians.

The summons by Jesus for his disciples to take up the cross was not the posing of a hypothetical; it was the warning of an inevitable. Daniel Berrigan, jailed repeatedly for acts of conscience, rightly says, "The geography of faith leads to the cross." We seek a different geography. One that would protect our lives and our families. One that would guard our security and our privilege.

Dietrich Bonhoeffer, martyred by the Nazis for his resistance to Hitler, was not being metaphorical when he wrote: "Whenever Christ calls us, his call leads us to death."[2] Over against this courageous claim, consider this old saying: "Everybody wants to go to heaven, but nobody wants to die." We are caught between these two truths: the truth of the cross of discipleship and the truth of our aversion to suffering and our fear of death. We want to be faithful to our Lord and to the kingdom of God while denying that the cross is also for us to bear. The point comes for each of us when we must make a decision. Will we follow where heart and conscience lead, regardless of personal risk, or will we save our lives and lose our souls in the process? We cannot hide from this question under the rubric of self-interest. The capacity to move forward toward a just society hinges on the willingness of thousands to suffer and to sacrifice, to pay the cost of conscience and the price of freedom.

"Militant mass action"—this part of Mandela's triadic formula is rejected out of hand by most Christians in the United States. We are too nice, too conciliatory, too privileged to want anything to do with mass action, particularly if it seems militant. We would like to convince the opposition with reason and with appeal to morality. We would like to preach the kingdom of God into existence. We need to hear again the timeless truth of Frederick Douglass: "Those who profess to favor freedom, and yet deprecate agitation, are men who want crops without plowing the ground. They want rain without thunder and lightning. They want the ocean without the awful roar of its many waters. The struggle may be a moral one, or it may be a physical one, or it may be both. But it must be a struggle. Power concedes nothing without demand; it never has, and it never will."

The point is not to be militant for the sake of being militant or to wear some macho badge of courage. The point is to be willing to act on a level that is commensurate with the injustices that we see. The point is not to swallow our anger, not to take the edge off our passion, not to soften our conscience. Christians must temper militancy with nonviolence but they must be willing to be as confrontational as Jesus.

Or as confrontational as Martin Luther King, Jr., whose last, greatest dream, was a Poor Peoples Campaign designed to force Congress to enact an Economic Bill of Rights that would have essentially eliminated poverty in this nation. Dr. King envisioned three phases to this campaign. Phase one was to be a rally of hundreds of thousands of people, the largest march ever to occur in the nation's capitol. In phase two, hundreds of thousands of poor people and their allies would disrupt federal agencies for three months or longer with militant acts of nonviolent civil disobedience that would swell the jails. If Congress still did not act, phase three would be launched involving nationwide boycotts of selected industries, sit-ins at factories, and civil disobedience throughout the country. With the assassination of Dr. King during the preliminary organizing for the Poor Peoples Campaign, the campaign turned into disarray as did so much of the remnant of the civil rights movement.

"Meticulous organization"—Christians have understood the necessity of this hard, disciplined work since the days of the early church. The mission of the church cannot be carried out in any sustained fashion without structure, without trained leaders, without a networking of relationships, and without substantial money. Congregation-based community organizing succeeds only with ongoing attentiveness to the formation of core teams, to the development of clergy caucuses, to the training of leadership, to the organizing of money, to the professional staffing of strategic campaigns, to the linking of regional organizations into a powerful, national network.

Here two truths engage each other. The first is a biblical truth: where there is no vision, the people perish (Prov. 29:18). The second is a historical truth: without organization, the vision perishes. Vision without organization is fanciful. Organization without vision is moribund. To become realized, a vision must be organized. To remain dynamic, an organization must be visionary. Congregation-based community organizing needs both vision bearers and organization builders. It is not enough to forge a vision. An organization must be created that can embody and engender that vision.

Here we do well to consider the biblical paradigm of creation, which joins together vision and organization. "In the beginning when God created the heavens and the earth, the earth was a formless void and darkness covered the face of the deep. . . . Then God said, 'Let there be light'; and there was light. And God saw that the light was good; and God separated the light from the darkness" (Gen. 1:1-4). The Hebrew creation story is not creation *ex nihil*, out of nothing. It is the ordering of chaos. It is shaping a formless void into light and darkness, heaven and earth, lands and oceans, sun and stars, animals and birds, men and women. Creation is the extraordinary joining of God's vision and God's organization.

What does the Gospel of John call this organizing power of God? The *Logos*. In the beginning was the *Logos*, and the *Logos* was with God, and the *Logos* was God. He was in the beginning with God. All things were created through the *Logos*, and without the *Logos* was not anything made which was made (John 1:1-3). The *Logos*, which is usually weakly translated as "the Word," is a concept in Greek philosophy that has to do with order, discipline, form, and definition. The *Logos* undergirds all of reality and gives every expression of reality its shape and meaning. Without *Logos* there is chaos and emptiness. For John, Christ Jesus is the *Logos*.

Another force is active in creation. In Greek mythology *Eros*, the god of love, arose to create the world. Everything was unmoving and silent. Then *Eros* emerged, with fire and heat, with passion and desire, and charged creation with life, with joy, with movement. Through *Eros* runs a permanent path toward the higher, the more beautiful, the more true, the more just, and the more human.[3] *Eros*, as a force, drives creation forward and upward. As Christians, we may rush here to supplant *Eros* with *Agape*. But let us stay with *Eros* for a bit and see what we might learn.

Leonardo Boff, in his book *St. Francis*, sees a dialectic at work between *Eros* and *Logos* (with reference, not to Christ, but to the ordering principle of Greek philosophy).[4] This dialectic is similar to the dialectic at work between vision and organization. Without *Eros*, the ordering and defining function of *Logos* becomes domination, repression, subjugation. *Logos* without *Eros* is reason without feeling. It is cold pragmatism. Similarly, *Eros* without *Logos* is dangerous. It is desire out of control. It is enthusiasm without purpose. It is energy without direction. Boff says that the *Logos* is for *Eros* what the retaining wall is for the immensity of waters behind a dam. Only because of that wall can the waters move the turbines and generate energy to light our cities. Together *Eros* and *Logos* provide a synergy that is both creative and life giving.

Vision bearers draw on *Eros*. Organization builders draw on *Logos*. Both are essential. Without a healthy synergy of the two, we run into trouble. When we have *Eros* without *Logos*, we may have lots of passion and vision but no organizing principle, nothing that offers shape and form. We may end up with a lot of passionate rhetoric about injustice but without any systematic approach to change.

In Milwaukee a group of inner-city clergy with a lot of *Eros* but no *Logos* took a public action. On opening day of the baseball season, this group leafleted outside of County Stadium demanding that the Milwaukee Brewers give 75 percent of their profits to alleviate poverty. What were the odds of getting that demand met? *Eros* without *Logos*. Passion that ends up going nowhere. After several subsequent press conferences, having no viable organization, the group disbanded.

A friend of mine, a well-known Jesuit priest, was once asked to sign a petition of "Outrage" by a left-wing extremist group. He read through the wild language of the petition and said, "I don't understand. What is it that you are outraged about?" "Everything," they said. "We want you to sign a petition of general outrage." *Eros* without *Logos*.

Eros has its positive side to be sure. Movement politics is filled with *Eros*, its passion, enthusiasm, vision, excitement. The very word *movement* suggests all of these elements. Given all that *Eros*, it is not surprising that movement politics has a certain romantic appeal. But without *Logos*, movement politics at best makes a limited, single-issue contribution to history and then fades off the screen.

Logos without *Eros* is no better. Here is something we wish would fade off the screen. *Logos* without *Eros* is at work in those organizations that long ago lost their vision and their passion. I remember serving on the Board of the Jersey City Branch of the NAACP. Here was a highly segregated city with a brutal police force, a Machiavellian mayor, a collapsing infrastructure, a failing school system, an environmental nightmare, a drug haven. And what did we do at our meetings? We listened as the secretary read every word of every single piece of correspondence, including form letters, since the last meeting. We heard long financial reports. We planned the annual banquet. On our better days we issued a letter of protest. *Logos* without *Eros*.

We must admit that the tendency to move toward *Logos* without *Eros* seems to be built into the nature of organizations. When congregation-based community organizations are young, the passion and enthusiasm are contagious; a fire fills the air. The media and politicians take note, perhaps with alarm, of this new, emerging force. But, over time, when the kingdom of God does not arrive, leadership on task forces and core teams begins to tire and dwindle. The organization takes on bureaucratic weight and bureaucratic style. Many people, once committed, return to the banality of individualized existence, to TV sets and computer screens.

Perhaps this movement from *Eros* to *Logos* in the life of organizations reflects the same movement in the life of a person. Children and adolescents are filled with *Eros*. They experience life with passion and a freshness of spirit. To a child, the adult world is dreadful, overwhelmed by the *Logos* of work, duty, responsibility, seriousness, with little or no time for play. For adults, particularly those carrying parental and professional responsibilities, *Eros* yields to *Logos*. The resulting orderliness may be useful and pragmatic but it is also stultifying to the spirit. The *Logos* represses and dominates those emotions that may threaten one's career or one's marriage or one's role as parent. It is the cost of a responsible, adult life. But within our souls remains a longing for the *Eros* of youth.

The following poem is about the *Eros* of romantic love fading into the *Logos* of institutionalized marriage. But it speaks also to the *Eros* of passion for justice fading into the *Logos* of organizing that has become institutionalized:

> They are not long the weeping and the laughter,
> love, desire, and hate.
> I think they have no portion in us
> once we pass the gate.
> They are not long, the days of wine and roses.
> Out of a misty dream our path emerges for awhile
> and then closes within a dream.[5]

As we build our organizations, how do we fuel our *Eros*? I think of prayer, relationships, anger, conscience, and action. When our work is rooted in prayer, we are connected to the source of our vision and to the One who energizes us for justice ministry. When we allow ourselves to enter more fully into relationships within our organization, we enter into a deeper level of commitment for the long haul. Solidarity releases the *Eros*. If we truly love and care for the people of our congregations and parish neighborhoods, we become angry when we see their humanity assaulted by brutal systems and unjust situations. This anger is a significant and useful expression of *Eros*. If we act on the basis of conscience, we feel more alive, whole, and integral. When we engage in actions that require some risk and courage, the *Eros* flows. Action is indeed the oxygen of an organization.

But *Eros* also needs *Logos*. Without its organization, the vision perishes. Much of congregation-based community organizing depends on the rather mundane work of doing one-on-ones, recruiting congregations, training leadership, raising money, developing judicatory relationships, conducting essential meetings, creating core teams, strengthening the clergy caucus. Without disciplined attentiveness to such details, an organization fades or never even blooms. We need the synergy. *Eros* and *Logos*. Passion and organization. A vision without which we perish and an organization without which the vision perishes.

Perhaps a closing anecdote from the life of St. Francis may be instructive. I tell it as it is recorded in Leonardo Boff's book about this beloved saint.[6] Francis was pure *Eros*, pure passionate vision. He drove the canon lawyers nuts. It took them years to get Francis to write a Rule for the Order of Friars Minor. His first draft was just a collection of Bible verses from the Sermon on the Mount. The one they finally accepted was only a few pages long. Francis simply wanted to live as Jesus had lived.

In 1209 Francis traveled to Rome to meet with Pope Innocent III to seek approval and authority for the creation of his order. The *Eros* of Francis needed the *Logos* of Innocent III or the vision would not be lived out within an order. Now Pope Innocent III was pure *Logos*, an organizational man, a power broker who had moved as far from the simplicity of Jesus as Francis had moved toward it. Under the papacy of Innocent III, the Catholic Church attained its highest secular power — more than half the lands of Europe were ecclesiastical holdings. For whatever reasons, Innocent III gave Francis his blessing. The Order of Friars Minor was formed. And for this, Francis, the man of *Eros*, was eternally grateful to Innocent III, the man of *Logos*.

In 1216 Pope Innocent III died. The pope who had become the sovereign of kings and princes was now laid in state before the high altar of a cathedral in Perugia. His body was covered in furs, vestments, jewels, gold, silver, every symbol of the double power and glory, secular and sacred that he had achieved. At midnight, long after the procession of the high, the mighty, and the lowly had paid their respects, the pope was left alone in the darkness. Thieves came into the cathedral and stripped the body of all the furs, vestments, gold, silver, and jewels. The body, already decaying, was left naked and alone.

But not entirely alone. Francis had hidden in a dark corner of the cathedral to watch, pray, and spend the night. When the thieves left, he took off his worn and dirty tunic, a tunic of penance that his friend Pope Innocent III had authorized him to wear in 1209, and with it he covered the naked body of the pope.

To the end *Eros* is the friend of *Logos*, and *Logos* is in need of *Eros*. Vision and organization.

We need both.

CHAPTER 11

Community

"Now the whole group of those who believed were of one heart and soul, and no one claimed private ownership of any possessions, but everything they owned was held in common. With great power the apostles gave their testimony to the resurrection of the Lord Jesus, and great grace was upon them all. There was not a needy person among them, for as many as owned lands or houses sold them and brought the proceeds of what was sold. They laid it at the apostles' feet, and it was distributed to each as any had need. There was a Levite, a native of Cyprus, Joseph, to whom the apostles gave the name Barnabus (which means 'son of encouragement'). He sold a field that belonged to him, then brought the money, and laid it at the apostles' feet." (Acts 4:32-37)

Biblical scholars are skeptical about the depth of communitarian sharing experienced in the early church. Some suggest that Barnabus is named as an exemplary exception rather than as the normative example. In their view, Luke is portraying an idyllic community in these verses; the more likely reality is the flawed community hinted at by the account of Ananias and Sapphira, which directly follows in Acts 5.

I tend to be a skeptic myself. The fact is that I don't sufficiently trust the power of the Holy Spirit to transform lives and to create authentic community. And so I was deservedly blown away by what I experienced a few years ago when I traveled to Tanzania on sabbatical with several members of the congregation that I serve. We arrived, blurry-eyed, at Kilimanjaro airport on a Saturday evening. Early the next morning a Land Rover took us, still blurry-eyed and also disoriented, about a mile and a half up the side of Mt. Kilimanjaro to worship at Lole Lutheran Parish. The cinder block sanctuary was packed with people, as it always is. Some of the congregants had walked miles to get to church, as they do every Sunday.

By U.S. standards, these Tanzanians are desperately poor. And yet the offering plates were filled with paper bills and coins. At the end of the worship service, a brass band (enthusiastic but of questionable quality) led the congregation out of the sanctuary and into the courtyard of the church. Before us, on the ground, were small bundles of firewood, onions, bananas, and various vegetables that I didn't recognize. For the next hour or so these items were auctioned off. The proceeds were placed in offering envelopes and given to the church counters.

A pastor from the diocese explained to me what was going on: "These are the gifts of the poor to the church. They have no money to give, so each Sunday they bring their produce. It's auctioned off, and this becomes their offering to the church. It's right out of biblical experience. These poor people, out of their poverty, are giving everything that they have." Little of the money is kept for the local church. (The pastor of Lole Lutheran Parish is paid about $30 per month. He raises cattle and plants a garden to feed his family.) From such sacrificial sharing, the Tanzanian church provides its impoverished society with essential services of health care, education, and vocational training. This radical sharing of limited resources is only one expression of the deep communitarian spirit of the Tanzanian church.

My experience of the depths of sharing, mutual love, exuberant faith, and total devotion to their Lord among the Tanzanian Christians whom I encountered made me feel as though I had entered into the early church of Acts 4. The truth is that the power of the Holy Spirit to create radical community is real and active. My skepticism about the communitarian nature of the early church is more an expression of my experience of the church in the United States than it is an honest exegesis of the texts in the book of Acts.

The church in the United States lacks community. The American church by and large is privatistic, insular, and individualistic. It reflects American culture. What is trumpeted as community is in actuality a series of bland and banal potluck dinners, or pseudo-psychological small groups, or introspective and innocuous Bible studies. The so-called community of the American church is most often a social setting for reinforcing the false values of a privileged society. Hugs, handshakes, and hallelujahs may be emotionally invigorating but they are hardly a substitute for the community that invites the Word of God to divide soul and spirit, bone and marrow, exposing our complicities and compromises.

"I believe in the Holy Spirit, the holy catholic Church, the communion of saints. . . ." This credal proclamation will not let us rest. It is a bold assertion of what we claim to be a present reality. It is a summons to community that challenges our customary experience of church. It is a faithful reminder that the Holy Spirit strives to gather and sanctify the people of God through an experience of community that defies all those centripetal forces of society that split and divide.

In the relatively new experiment in faith called congregation-based community organizing, I see hope for creating biblical community within the Christian church in the United States. Such community must be measured by the historic marks of what it means to be the church. Christian community must be distinctive from generic community, which could be defined as a group of people who understand that their destiny is intertwined. After all, street gangs, the Mafia, and cults may well understand that the destiny of their respective membership is intertwined; to this extent it must be admitted that those in these groups do experience community. But what does it mean to be the communion of saints? What makes Christian community Christian? The historic marks of the Church are helpful here: the Christian community is called to be holy, catholic, apostolic, and confessional. Congregation-based community organizing contributes to the creation of precisely such community.

Holy. The word makes us look elsewhere. The word seems best reserved for God or for the church triumphant in heaven. How can the creeds claim this word for the church on earth? Why do we keep using this word after the Constantinian compromise, after the Crusades, after the Inquisition, after centuries of imperialistic evangelism, after the failure of the church during slavery, after the acquiescence of the church during Nazi Germany, after the violent division of Christians in Northern Ireland, after the slaughter of Muslims in Bosnia, after. . . . The litany of failure is so long that it would force the word *holy* into heaven. And yet it remains. I believe in the holy catholic Church.

Is it easier to apply the word *holy* to the local church? Any pastor knows the frailty of his or her congregation. I have seen parishioners go to prison for homicide, armed robbery, and theft. I know painfully well the intractable hold of drug and alcohol addictions on some parishioners. I have seen families in such bitter feuds that they refuse to worship together. I recall a fellow pastor complaining of baptizing a man only to learn that he mercilessly beat his wife a few hours later. My own moral failures drive me to my knees.

I believe in the *holy* catholic church. The historic failure of the church, of the local congregation, and of the individual Christian is not the only word to be spoken here. The reality also holds the faithful voices of conscience rising up from the church throughout history: the blood of the martyrs, the costly compassion of the saints, the testimony that the local congregation is the last vestige of hope in many devastated urban communities, and the reality that many faithful Christians continue to struggle with the claim of the Word of God on their lives over the culture in which they live.

To be holy is to be set apart for God's purposes. If the Christian community is to be holy, then it must understand itself as set apart, as distinctive from the prevailing culture. The Christian community cannot be a mirror image of the culture. The Christian community cannot undergird the false values of the culture. In short, the Christian community must be prophetic. The Word of God must be proclaimed by the Christian community with a clarity that challenges the ruinous words of the culture.

Congregation-based community organizing forces the church out of its somnolence and into the public arena. It draws congregations together and into public stands over against prevailing powers and oppressive systems. It is controversial. It challenges the church to take risks and to act with courage. Congregations engaged in this kind of organizing are indeed set apart for God's purposes. They are instruments of justice and agents of deliverance. They are bearers of the Word of God into the world. In this regard, they are holy.

Congregation-based community organizations are emerging in virtually every major city in the United States. The congregations that comprise these organizations have a distinctive understanding of what it means to be set apart for God's purposes, what it means to be holy in a society that seeks to subvert and infiltrate the gospel (as it has done so well in the defection of many Christians to the prosperity gospel). The clergy and laity who lead these organizations are the unsung prophets of contemporary America. They sweat it out amidst the daily brutalities of urban poverty. They stand against powerful opposition. They trust each other and believe in God. They and their communities are, in my judgment, holy.

Sartre proposed that existence precedes essence. We are not born with meaning. It takes an act of courage to create meaning out of our lives. This idea is, I think, the reality we encounter in the Christian church. Holiness is not an attribute of a congregation by virtue of its existence. Claiming that we have been made holy does not make us so. It takes courageous action to bring forth holiness from the church or from the individual Christian. Such action is of course always a sign of God's active grace. We do not make ourselves holy through any sort of works righteousness. Our being made holy is, nonetheless, a result of action, not of an *a priori* claim about who we are. I cannot claim to be set apart for God's purposes unless I act as if I am. Congregation-based community organizing provides a vehicle for such action.

I believe in the holy *catholic* church. The universality of the church is, indeed, a wonder. Christians who travel across oceans and continents will encounter their brothers and sisters in the faith. Every Sunday the gospel is proclaimed through word and song in hundreds of different languages throughout the earth. The eucharist draws to the altar people of every color and culture, of every ability and disability, of every nation and race. The church catholic defies every human division.

But what about the local Christian community? How does it embody the church catholic? Here and there Christian communities are blessed with marvelous diversity. I have a friend who pastored a church in New York City whose membership encompassed thirty-four primary languages. It is a joy to worship in such congregations. To hear different languages. To see different skin colors. To sense the rhythm of various cultures.

But such an experience is the exception. Homogeneity is the rule. Usually we encounter in the local congregation a church that is exclusively or predominantly black or white, English speaking or Spanish speaking, privileged or poor. We see churches separated by denominational divisions, by opposing claims to sole possession of the truth, by the new nondenominationalism, which is in essence a strict denial of the church catholic.

Ecumenical dialogues seek to restore the catholicity of the church that has been shattered into hundreds of denominations. Theologians debate, discuss, and draft documents in a rarefied atmosphere remote from the daily experience of the local church. Where progress is happening, it is slow and uncertain. And in any case, these ecumenical ventures are simply not designed to deal with the racial and class divisions in the church catholic, which are as damaging as any theological rifts.

Here again congregation-based community organizing offers a hopeful sign. Churches engaged in this venture have no choice but to abandon their parochialism and mute their denominational claims. Most congregation-based community organizations are comprised of churches representing at least a dozen different denominations. Public meetings of these organizations offer a beatific vision. Where else can you see a spirited gathering of a thousand or more Christians of various denominations, black and white, Latino and Anglo, Asian American and Native

American, middle class and poor, praying together, singing together, calling public officials into accountability, proclaiming victories on various justice issues?

Lay leaders working on task forces and pastors active in clergy caucuses of congregation-based community organizations are blessed with the opportunity to build authentic relationships across racial and class lines. It is slow, sometimes delicate work. It takes time to replace mutual suspicions with mutual trust. Gradually, presumptions and prejudices are found to be false. The unity of brotherhood and sisterhood in the Christian faith is joyfully discovered to be preeminent. Friendships are formed. Community is experienced. The church catholic is honored.

An ecumenical dialogue occurs within the clergy caucuses of congregation-based community organizing. It is usually not formal. It may lack theological precision. But it is genuine. The flavor of this ecumenical dialogue is positive and celebratory. The discovery is made that denominational differences may not be all that bad; in fact they have offered the opportunity for diverse gifts to be shaped within the church catholic. These clergy caucuses honor the lyrical style of Baptist preachers, the sacramental devotion of Roman Catholic and Episcopalian priests, the exegetical training of Lutheran pastors, the personal piety of Pentecostal pastors, and so on. The result is not syncretistic. Baptists remain Baptists. Lutherans remain Lutherans. Roman Catholics remain Roman Catholics. But the faith and practice of each are positively influenced and nuanced by experience of the other. And, beneath it all, is the recognition that, regardless of denominational persuasion, we are all embraced by the church catholic.

The Christian community is called to be *apostolic*. Historically, this call has been linked to the claim of spiritual authority based on apostolic succession, to an unbroken continuum of ordinations traced to the apostles, to faithful conformity to the teachings of the early apostles. Given this understanding of what it means to be apostolic, congregation-based community organizing has little contribution to make.

But what if we were to understand apostolic on a different level? In the early church, an apostle was one who had a personal experience of the risen Christ and who was sent to proclaim the good news. In Greek, the word for apostle means "the one who is sent." By this measure, the Christian community is apostolic when it has encountered the resurrected Christ and when it is bold in proclaiming the good news of the resurrection. The experience and proclamation of the resurrected Christ are always within a historical context and always over against the realities and forces of death. The resurrection is not a break from human history but God's redemption of it. The resurrection of Christ is not an individual defeat of death; it is a universal conquest of death and all its minions.

The apostolic church is so transformed by its encounter with the risen Christ that it boldly proclaims the victory of life in the midst of death. I had a sense of what this encounter means when I visited Buchenwald concentration camp while on a visit to Germany. Amidst the horrific gloom of that death camp, I learned the story of the martyrdom of one of the prisoners, a Lutheran pastor. (I recall his name as Paul Schneider. May the saints forgive my feeble memory.) Early one Easter morning, Pastor Schneider stood up in his tiny cell and shouted through the barred window into the courtyard of Buchenwald, "Christ is risen." The prison guards rushed in and beat him mercilessly. When they left, he stood up and shouted again through the window, "Christ is risen." The guards entered his cell and broke both his legs. When they left, somehow he got his hands up to the bars of the window, pulled himself up, and shouted once more into the courtyard, "Christ is risen." This time the guards charged into his cell and beat him to death.

Death claims urban America for itself. Death by street violence. Death by drugs. Death by an infant mortality rate as high as that in Third World countries. The death of uneducated minds. The death of decaying neighborhoods. The death of decimated families. The death of joblessness. The death of dreams. Into the courtyard of such death, congregation-based community organizing proclaims the resurrection of Christ, the unbending hope in the power of life, the unyielding belief that God, not death, has the last word. It is an apostolic proclamation.

Kandinsky, in his book *Concerning the Spiritual in Art*, offers a theory of cultural progress that utilizes the image of a moving arrowhead—the broad part of the arrowhead always ends up where the narrow point has led. Artistic geniuses are like the point of the arrrowhead. Even though in their lifetime their contributions may be controversial, misunderstood, perhaps rejected, over time their cutting edge achievements are integrated into the broader culture.

Congregation-based community organizing offers an apostolic "point of the arrow" for the urban church in this country. Churches engaged in this life-giving enterprise are cutting edge. They lead the recalcitrant portion of the urban church forward, toward the coming kingdom of God. They enjoy a clarity of mission, a sense of being "sent" that is inspired by their encounter with the risen Christ.

Finally, the Christian community is called to be *confessional*. The historic creeds define the parameters of the church. The church makes specific claims about God, about Jesus Christ, about the Holy Spirit, about forgiveness, about the resurrection of the dead. The Christian community consists of those who stake their lives on these claims. The confessional witness of the Christian community, at its best, makes these claims over against the false claims of the dominant culture.

Such was the experience of the early church when it proclaimed that "Jesus is Lord." The Roman Caesars claimed the title "Lord" (*Dominus*) for themselves. For Christians to claim the Lordship of Jesus was to contradict the lordship of Caesar. The rite of induction into the Roman military included offering a pinch of incense to a statue of Caesar. For early Christians, this act was one of idolatry. They knew and worshiped only one Lord. They refused to divide their loyalties between Christ and Caesar, church and state. For this reason they were held suspect, persecuted, and martyred.

In 1934 the Barmen Declaration of the Confessing Church in Germany proclaimed the Lordship of Jesus over against the false claims to lordship being made by Hitler and the Nazis. The signers of that proclamation were eventually imprisoned, exiled, or executed. When the atomic bomb was dropped on Hiroshima, Dorothy Day warned that the Lordship of Jesus was being challenged by the lordship of the Bomb. Some Christians who heeded that warning ended up in prison for their acts of conscientious resistance to the nuclear build-up.

Congregation-based community organizing is confessional when it proclaims the Lordship of Jesus over against the lordship of those institutions, principalities, and systems that diminish and destroy the lives of the poor. It is confessional when it makes this proclamation public with words and actions that are unequivocal, courageous, and conscientious. The false lords of this world are quite content to have the Lordship of Jesus proclaimed liturgically and privatistically within the confines of the sanctuary. To make this proclamation with boldness in the public arena is quite a different matter.

Dietrich Bonhoeffer distinguished between the confession of faith in liturgy and the confessional stance of the church in the world. The liturgical confession of faith distinguishes the Christian community from those who are undecided or opposed to the Word of God. The confession of faith in worship announces the stance of a Christian before God in response to God's Word of truth. The confessional stance of the church in the world is different. It is not the profession of a religion over against the godless. "The primary confession of the Christian before the world is the deed which interprets itself. . . . The deed alone is our confession of faith before the world."[1]

The confessional failure of the Christian church in the public arena has clearly not been its silence about Jesus. It has been vocal. At times it has been vociferous, badgering, and abusive in its use of words. The confession of faith that is so truthful in liturgy often becomes distorted into propaganda over against the godless when announced in the world. The world needs, not more words from the church, but truthful action, "the deed which interprets itself." Congregation-based community organizing attempts to offer such actions, such deeds in urban America. Now and then Christians engaged in organizing act with such clarity that their deeds interpret themselves as deeds consistent with the Word of God in history. It is then that congregation-based community organizing is truly confessional.

CHAPTER 12

A Spirituality for the Long Haul

"As for me, I am already being poured out as a libation, and the time of my departure has come. I have fought the good fight, I have finished the race, I have kept the faith. From now on there is reserved for me the crown of righteousness, which the Lord, the righteous judge, will give me on that day, and not only to me but also to all who have longed for his appearing." (2 Tim. 4:6-8)

The summons to do justice is an invitation into an interesting life, into an unleashing of one's inner power, into authentic community, into the possibility of fulfillment in a vacuous society. But it must also be admitted that, at times, the summons to do justice feels like a life sentence. Dorothy Day spoke of the "harsh and dreadful love" demanded of her in her "long loneliness" of struggle for justice and devotion to the poor. No pursuit of justice is undertaken without sacrifice, risk, and loss. A cloud of emotional heaviness may descend. Now and again the temptation surfaces to give up, to abandon the struggle, to seek instead a life of normalcy, ease, and security for oneself and one's family. After all, one has to contend with the tentative nature of any "victories" in the public arena and the obdurate nature of systemic evil. An added pain comes from seeing the "righteous" in the struggle caught up in petty outbursts and displays of vain ego. And an additional aspect is the unhappy discovery of one's own limitations, cowardice, and mediocrity.

Amidst such realities, what keeps one going year after year, decade after decade? For those who have been summoned to do justice, the Spirit simply will not let go. The lament of Jeremiah puts it this way: "O Lord, you have enticed me, and I was enticed; you have overpowered me, and you have prevailed. . . . For the word of the Lord has become for me a reproach and derision all day long. If I say, 'I will not mention him, or speak any more in his name,' then within me there is something like a burning fire shut up in my bones; I am weary with holding it in, and I cannot" (Jer. 20:7-9). Those summoned to do justice would like a more normal life, easier laughter, fewer burdens to carry. But always they feel "something like a burning fire" in their bones that cannot be contained.

Like it or not, those summoned to do justice must carry this burden. Like the prophets of God, they see and feel the world differently from others. Perhaps no one has described this prophetic experience as clearly and poetically as Rabbi Abraham Heschel:

> The world is a proud place, full of beauty, but the prophets are scandalized, and rave as if the whole world were a slum. To us, a single act of injustice—cheating in business, exploitation of the poor—is slight; to the prophets, a disaster. To us, injustice is injurious to the welfare of the people; to the prophets, a deathblow to existence; to us, an episode; to them, a catastrophe, a threat to the world. . . .
>
> The prophet is a person who feels fiercely. God has thrust a burden upon his soul, and he is bowed and stunned before humanity's fierce greed. Frightful is the agony of humankind; no human voice can convey its full terror. Prophecy is the voice that God has lent to silent agony, a voice to the plundered poor, to the profaned riches of the world.[1]

It seems that those whom God summons to do justice have no choice but to act on their calling unless they are capable of denying the way that they see the world, belying their integrity, and resisting the Spirit that sets their inner being on fire. But what sustains them? Organizers are fond of saying that "action is the oxygen of an organization." Without question, action on behalf of justice can be exhilarating. Action deepens the bonding and sense of community among those involved, especially if the action requires some risk. Action relieves the inner pressure of conscience to take a bold stand. On those occasions when action actually produces results there is a sense of accomplishment.

But action can also be frenetic, mindless, and damaging to the human spirit. The activist can get seduced into becoming a mirror image of the culture that he or she is resisting, succumbing to the illusions of power, ego, and presumed influence. Action can be a whirlwind that swoops down upon the soul of a person and sends her or his life into a crazy spin. One can become addicted to action and lose one's marriage, one's children, one's balance, one's soul.

Here we need to be reminded that action must not take away one's humanity, that action must remain on the human scale of things, that not only must a prophetic "no" to social injustice be spoken, but a prophetic "yes" to life must be proclaimed. We refer back to Jeremiah where, in chapter 32, Jerusalem is under siege by the Babylonian army and the prophet Jeremiah is in custody for undermining the war effort. Amidst these momentous events comes an interlude and much is made of what seems to be a minor transaction—the purchase of a field at Anathoth. This simple, human action by the prophet does nothing to lift the siege or to soften the heart of King Zedekiah or to impede the mad rush toward national disaster. And yet it is a powerful, hopeful action. It is a prophetic yes. The meaning of the action may not be understood for many years. And so the God of Israel instructs the prophet: "Take these deeds, both this sealed deed of purchase and this open deed, and put them in an earthenware jar, in order that they may last for a long time. For thus says the Lord of hosts, the God of Israel: Houses and fields and vineyards shall again be bought in this land" (Jer. 32:14-15).

The prophetic yes has a human scale, a human dimension. Jeremiah does not become a real estate developer. It is, after all, only a family field. We have here an image counter to the grand schemes of those at war and at the helms of power who demand and crave all. In contrast to the dominant culture that seeks to devour and consume without limit and elbows for ever-expanded power, prestige, influence, and wealth, the prophetic yes maintains a human dimension and an essential trust in the providence of God. The prophetic yes makes no claim to turn everything around, to solve all problems, to undo all injustices. The prophetic yes is not obsessed with results, does not seek to justify one's existence through activism, does not groom the activist's ego, does not build a monument to the activist's life. Jeremiah purchases a field and praises God. And in that human act God invests a word of hope: houses and fields and vineyards shall again be bought in this land.

The prophetic yes acknowledges that those summoned to do justice are invited into a human enterprise. We act, but we profess that the results of our actions are in larger hands than our own. We are not summoned to play God. A certain modesty about the significance of one's actions goes a long way in sustaining the one who acts. It does not diminish in any way the value of these actions. It is simply to admit that the measure of our "victories" and "successes" is that they are always relative and partial. And yet, as Rosemary Radford Ruether reminds us, "Concretely, the relative and partial good . . . is often the measure of survival for those who live on the margins."[2] In assessing the value of working for justice and change that is always relative, she recalls the wise saying of one of her friends who survived near starvation in Hungary during World

War II: "The difference between a haircut and a decapitation is only relative, but it is also the difference between life and death when it is your head."[3]

The prophetic yes of Jeremiah is life affirming. A field is purchased in the midst of a siege. So also those summoned to do justice are to affirm the giftedness of life even as they protest and seek to overturn the tragic, destructive, and often horrific dimensions of injustice. Art, music, children, flower gardens, parties, romantic love, fishing, sports, sunrises—the world is intended to be a veritable playground. Who needs or wants dour activist gloom? I recall a dinner party with some friends whose lives are devoted to justice and compassion for the poor. The conversation became intense and heavy, moving drearily around the globe with one horror story following another. Suddenly, my youngest daughter appeared dressed in a ballerina costume. "Does anybody know that I can dance?" she asked. No one noticed. The conversation continued uninterrupted. Emma Goldman was right: "If I can't dance, I don't want to be part of your revolution."

The prophetic yes seeks the Source of life that sustains the soul. John Dear, a Jesuit priest, author, and activist, recalls gathering with hundreds of people in the Nevada desert shortly after the Persian Gulf war to pray together and to commit civil disobedience in opposition to nuclear weapons testing. During the opening prayer, Daniel Berrigan sat on Dear's left and Jim Wallis on his right. After the prayer time, the organizers asked everyone to turn to those around them and discuss what they might do to oppose militarism. Berrigan and Wallis looked at John Dear. So he spoke first: "We need to reorganize the peace movement," he declared. "We need to mobilize people around the country to come forward by the thousands, eventually by the millions, to demand disarmament and justice. We need to wake people up to the realities of war and its destructive consequences for our nation." After going on at length in this fashion, Dear concluded, apparently much to the relief of Berrigan and Wallis. After a long pause, Berrigan turned to Dear and said quietly, "I just think we need to unleash the contemplative springs within."[4]

How do we unleash the contemplative springs within? Here is what sustains the soul, enables truthful perception of reality, guards our actions from false ego, keeps our lives in balance. Each of us needs to find our own way in the inner search for the life-giving, contemplative springs. Each of us is different. For me, the search for the contemplative springs within has led me into iconography. Perhaps it seems strange to conclude a book on congregation-based community organizing with references to iconography. I don't feel that way at all. My involvement in congregation-based community organizing began in 1985. It was the same year that I began studying iconography under the master iconographer Vladislav Andrejev at the School of Sacred Arts in Manhattan.

For me, congregation-based community organizing and iconography are parallel streams. One informs the other. Congregation-based community organizing strives to make the invisible ideal of the kingdom of God into a visible reality in accordance with the prayer of Jesus: Thy kingdom come, Thy will be done, *on earth* as it is in heaven. Icons are the invisible made visible. Andrejev says, "The icon is the breath of a pilgrim, a sojourner who is trying to enter into the kingdom of heaven." The intent of iconography is not for us to leave material reality in order to enter some idealized state of consciousness. Rather, icons invite us to encounter the spiritual dimension that undergirds all material reality and that must be reverenced if wholeness is to be experienced in the material realm. Congregation-based community organizing sees the image of God within people and works to release the giftedness and inner power that is so often abused and diminished by oppressive systems. Icons offer us a view of the restored image that is ours in Christ. The icon is an image that depicts the transfigured person and summons forth the potential saint that is in each of us.

In congregation-based community organizing the transformation of a person is a slow, deliberative process involving agitation, training, action, reflection, connection to community. In iconography, the transformation into a saint is signified particularly in the creation of the golden nimbus, the halo, around the sacred face. A difficult and demanding process is used, which is powerful in its symbolism. The iconographer applies several layers of red burnish clay to the desired area. Careful and laborious sanding and burnishing creates a mirror-smooth surface on the clay. This is the clay of our earthly nature (*Adam* means "clay" in Hebrew), which was created in God's image but, given the defilement of that image, needs the transformational activity of the Holy Spirit in order to be changed into the likeness of God.

When the surface of the clay has been prepared as perfectly as possible, the iconographer works one small section at a time, applying a little vodka, and then, breathing from deep within unto that section of the board, applies gold leaf. The spirit of the iconographer is breathed into the icon. The Spirit is that which transforms our clay into gold. According to Vladislav Andrejev, "Out of everything that is holy in an icon, the most ineffable presence is indicated by gold. Gold does not have any color. It signifies the Unapproachable Light. It is, so to speak, spiritual gold, which in an icon signifies the eternal, divine background of the whole of life. It is, therefore, the space of *true* reality."

Every aspect of the icon surface begins in darkness and moves, through a series of floatings and highlightings of pigments, toward light. Not only the halo and the face are subject to this rubric. Even the clothing and the background start with dark colors and move toward light. In the great icons, like those of Andrei Rublev, light pours through the halo, through the face, through the clothing. Symbolically, the icon enfleshes the transformation of darkness into light by the activity of the Holy Spirit. St. Symeon the New Theologian (tenth century) said, "God is Light, and those whom He makes worthy to see Him, see Him as Light; those who receive Him, receive Him as Light. This light without change, without decline and never extinguished, enlightens us; it speaks, it acts, it lives and gives life, it transforms into light those whom it illumines." Similarly, St. Gregory Palamas (fourteenth century) said, "Whoever participates in the divine energy becomes, to some extent, light; he is united to the light."

St. Seraphim, a Russian saint of the nineteenth century, once had a conversation with his disciple Motovilov in the clearing of a forest on a winter morning. When Motovilov asked St. Seraphim of Sarov about the purpose of the Christian life, the monk answered that it is the "acquisition of the Holy Spirit." "But what does this mean?" Motovilov persisted. "Look at me," Seraphim said to him simply. Then Motovilov saw his friend standing in the snow with his face more dazzling than the sun and his eyes shining like lightning.

Congregation-based community organizing, at its best, seeks the true reality in which the light of God shines through the darkness of injustice and human evil. It seeks to bring to light the potential of human beings to live as the children of God in just relationships. It seeks to end the night of human misery. It seeks the light of the kingdom of God. It seeks this light in individuals, in communities, and in society.

One of my favorite icons is the Holy Face, also known as the *Acheiropoietos* (the icon "made without hands"), which depicts the Face of our Lord on a cloth, a *mandilion*. The Holy Face icon has its origins in the legend of King Abgar of Edessa who lived at the time of Jesus and suffered from leprosy. Hearing that Jesus had great power to heal, King Abgar sent two of his officials to Jesus with a letter humbly seeking healing. Moved by the letter, Jesus pressed his face to a cloth and gave it to the officials to take back to Abgar. When Abgar unwrapped the cloth, he saw a miraculous image of the Face of Jesus and was instantly healed.

This power of the Holy Face to heal us is, in the first instance, a healing of the leprosy that has changed the face we were born with into a mask. Particularly in urban America we learn to wear a mask, to pretend to be someone that we are not, to hide our true face, our true feelings, our true identity. We speak of our *persona* (the theatrical mask in Greek theater). We show our *persona* to others as if it were who we are. Eventually, our true self is concealed even from us. Then we are lost.

One Latin word for mask is *larva*. In ancient times *larva* had the meaning of an astral corpse. The one in whom the image of God has become concealed by a mask is dead inside. A mask lies. It is false. It shows to others that which it is not. A major characteristic of a mask is false reality. We can know nothing of a person when we look through the face that has turned into a mask. A mask bears darkness. A mask is a face without a life in it, without spirit. We see the mask all around us. We see it in young people who kill for a coat or for the thrill of killing and who show in their eyes not the slightest feeling of remorse. We see the mask in drug addicts who speak of love while stealing the food money for their children. We see the mask in suburbanites who feign compassion while feeling condescension toward the poor. We see the mask in white Christians who conceal their racism. We see the mask in politicians, in businesspeople, in clergy. We are all practiced in the art of theater.

The Holy Face heals us and removes our mask, restores to us an authentic face. Gazing at the face of Christ, we rediscover our true face, which reveals our spiritual essence, the image of God within us. St. Paul speaks of this healing process: "And all of us, with unveiled faces, seeing the glory of the Lord as though reflected in a mirror, are being transformed into the same image from one degree of glory to another" (2 Cor. 3:18). Even those pronouncing the death sentence on Stephen saw that God had created a holy face in him: "And all who sat in the council looked intently at him, and they saw that his face was like the face of an angel" (Acts 6:15).

Congregation-based community organizing seeks to restore the human face freed of the masks imposed by racism and classism, freed of the masks worn to survive the streets of urban America, freed of the masks of victimization and self-deprecation. Congregation-based community organizing seeks authentic relationships based on mutual recognition and mutual regard.

An old rabbi once asked his students: "How do you know when the night is over and the day has dawned?" One student raised his hand. "Could it be, Rabbi, that it is when you look in the distance and see a tree and can tell whether it is a pear tree or an orange tree?" "No," said the rabbi. Another student raised his hand. "Could it be, Rabbi, that it is when you look in the distance and see an animal and can tell whether it is a dog or a bear?" "No," answered the rabbi. "Well, tell us then," implored the students. "Tell us how we can know when the night is over and the day has dawned." The old man responded, "It is when you can look into the face of any man or woman and see there the face of your brother or sister. Because, if you cannot do that, no matter how bright it is you are still in the night."

Early in the twentieth century the Soviet government allowed the Orthodox church to begin a painstaking process of restoring ancient icons. Some dated back four or five hundred years. They looked dark and gloomy. As the restoration work was done, an amazing discovery was made. Beneath the centuries-old soot from candle smoke and incense, the true colors of the icons were revealed as brilliant and bright. Icons embody a long-haul spirituality of beauty and joy.

Those summoned to do justice will get battered around in life. Over the decades the early idealism may be covered with the soot of repeated disappointment. The world as they experience it may actually seem a worse place now than when they began their struggle for justice years ago. But the Spirit who first summoned them will also fill them with light and grace. Deep within, deeper than any discouragement or defeat, deeper than any regret or resignation, there lie the beauty and the joy of a life well lived.

Following are the four national networks of congregation-based community organizations:

Direct Action and Research Training Center (DART)
John Calkins, Director
314 NE 26th Terrace
Miami, FL 33137
Phone: 305-576-8022
Web site: www.thedartcenter.org

The Gamaliel Foundation
Gregory Galluzzo, Director
203 N. Wabash Avenue, Suite 808
Chicago, IL 60601
Phone: 312-357-2639
Web site: www.gamaliel.org

Industrial Areas Foundation (IAF)
Ed Chambers, Director
220 W. Kinzie Street, 5th floor
Chicago, IL 60610
Phone: 312-245-9211
Web site (unofficial): www.tresser.com/IAF.htm

Pacific Institute for Community Organization (PICO)
John Baumann, S.J., Director
171 Santa Rosa Avenue
Oakland, CA 94610
Phone: 510-655-2801
Web site: www.pico.rutgers.edu

A primary funder of congregation-based community organizing and an excellent source for further information and contacts is the Catholic Campaign for Human Development:

Catholic Campaign for Human Development (CCHD)
3211 Fourth Street NE
Washington, DC 20017-1194
Phone: 202-541-3210
Web site: www.nccbuscc.org/cchd

NOTES

1. The World as It Is

1. Alexis de Tocqueville, *Democracy in America Volume II* (New York: Knopf, 1953), 318.

2. Daniel Berrigan, *Isaiah* (Minneapolis: Fortress, 1996), 34.

3. Engaging the Public Arena

1. What follows is drawn extensively from the review by Peter Steinfels, *The New York Times* (November 5, 1994, section 1, p. 12) of *The Unrelieved Paradox: Studies in the Theology of Franz Bibfeldt*, ed. Martin E. Marty and Jerald C. Brauer (Grand Rapids: Eerdmans, 1994).

2. Ibid.

4. Congregation-Based Community Organizing

1. See the overviews of congregation-based community organizing in Robert McClory, "Wherever Two or Three Thousand Are Gathered . . .," *U.S. Catholic* (March 2000); and Helene Slessarev, "Saul Alinsky Goes to Church," *Sojourners* (March–April 2000).

5. Power

1. William Stringfellow, *An Ethic for Christians and Other Aliens in a Strange Land* (Waco, Tex.: Word, 1973), 78.

2. Reinhold Niebuhr, *Moral Man and Immoral Society* (New York: Scribner's, 1960), 9.

3. Gerhard Kittel, *Theological Dictionary of the New Testament*, trans. and ed. Geoffrey W. Bromiley (Grand Rapids: Eerdmans, 1964), 291.

4. Karl Rahner, *Theological Investigations Vol. IV*, trans. Kevin Smyth (New York: Seabury, 1974), 396.

5. Norman K. Gottwald, *The Tribes of Yahweh* (Maryknoll, N.Y.: Orbis, 1979).

6. Walter Wink, *Naming the Powers* (Philadelphia: Fortress, 1984), 15.

7. J. Deotis Roberts, *Black Theology in Dialogue* (Philadelphia: Westminster, 1987), 86.

8. Dorothee Soelle, *Choosing Life* (Philadelphia: Fortress, 1981), 96.

9. Gregory A. Galluzzo, "Weekly Report," unpublished staff report, February 21, 1993.

10. Marianne Williamson, *A Return to Love* (New York: Harper-Collins, 1993), 190–91.

6. Self-Interest

1. Dante Alighieri, *The Inferno*, trans. John Ciardi (New York: Mentor, 1954), 42.

2. Cornel West, *Race Matters* (Boston: Beacon, 1993), 14.

7. One-on-Ones

1. Martin Buber, *I and Thou*, trans. Walter Kaufmann (New York: Scribner, 1970).

9. Metropolitan Organizing

1. The background material in this chapter is drawn extensively from Gregory A. Galluzzo, "Regionalism and Racism," unpublished article, 1998.

2. See David Rusk, *Cities without Suburbs*, 2d ed. (Baltimore, Md.: Johns Hopkins University Press, 1995) and *Inside Game/Outside Game* (Washington, D.C.: Brookings Institute Press, 1999).

3. See Myron Orfield, *Metropolitics* (Washington, D.C.: Brookings Institute Press, 1997).

10. Building and Sustaining an Organization

1. Nelson Mandela, *Long Walk to Freedom* (Boston: Little, Brown, 1994), 104.

2. Dietrich Bonhoeffer, *Discipleship*, trans. Barbara Green and Reinhard Krauss (Dietrich Bonhoeffer Works, vol. 4; Minneapolis: Fortress, 2001), 87.

3. Leonardo Boff, *St. Francis: A Model for Human Liberation*, trans. John W. Diercksmeier (New York: Crossroad, 1984), 12.

4. Ibid., 12–15.

5. *The Columbia Granger's Dictionary of Poetry Quotations*, ed. Edith P. Hazen (New York: Columbia University Press, 1992), 147.

6. Boff, *St. Francis*, 105–6.

11. Community

1. Dietrich Bonhoeffer, *A Testament to Freedom: The Essential Writings of Dietrich Bonhoeffer*, ed. Geffrey B. Kelly and F. Burton Nelson (San Francisco: HarperSanFrancisco, 1995), 86.

12. A Spirituality for the Long Haul

1. Abraham Joshua Heschel, *The Prophets* (New York: Harper & Row, 1962), 3–5.

2. Rosemary Radford Ruether, "One of the Great Truth-Tellers," in John Dear, S.J., ed., *Apostle of Peace: Essays in Honor of Daniel Berrigan* (Maryknoll, N.Y.: Orbis, 1996), 45.

3. Ibid.

4. John Dear, S.J., "An Introduction (of Sorts)," in Dear, ed., *Apostle of Peace*, 15.

Faith communities—Christian, Jewish, Muslim, and others—dot the landscape of every city in the United States, large and small. The majority of these congregations have just several handfuls of people committed to the "mission of the church." For many of the others the purpose of the church is nebulous or rooted in the generally good values of the culture. The distinctive voice of the church is rarely heard.

The increased pluralism and secularization of society are but two factors that challenge the existence of these institutions that seem more an ode to the past than a painting of the future. But somehow, someway these groups of people continue to "keep on keepin' on." They remain one of the few institutions left in the heart of our major cities. They are places where exciting things are happening in some cases. In-depth renewal of faith communities may well be happening in places that seem the weakest. The Christian Scriptures, at least, recognize that out of what the world calls weakness comes strength.

Some supporters of these congregations seem to think that just because faith communities have been around, they will continue to be around. Others see these communities as created by the Spirit of God and therefore off limits to forces of destruction.

But perhaps the relative longevity of the church, at least of the Christian so-called mainline congregations, lies more in the record of the past than in the promise of the future. Perhaps it is the history of the church that we continue to celebrate and not its role in coming days. Its role as a power in that culture is now waning, and there is just enough momentum generated in times past to keep the machine ticking ahead as we open the twenty-first century.

Certainly the dream of those who named the twentieth century "The Christian Century" did not come true. Our awakening to a whole new world community in this century has made it clear that domination by any one group, however desirable, is not possible. The Christian church will forever be a minority in the world no matter how many "mega" churches we build. The sum total of those congregations' memberships multiplied twenty times over is still an infinitesimal percentage when compared with the world population. The point is that the church based on the good news of the Christian Scriptures can never use numerical growth as its singular or primary measure of worth. So we must ask, What is the central aim and function of the faith community in our day?

In *Doing Justice* Dennis Jacobsen has captured the central purposes of the gathered Christian community. Under a description of congregation-based community organizing, Jacobsen points to one strong and practical tool for fulfilling the mission of the church.

Jacobsen writes with passion for congregation-based organizing. The author also writes with sensitivity to the precariousness of any undertaking. He is strong in his persuasion, but he is not inflexible. This quality makes his book accessible to all and valuable for dialogue among all those who want to release the gifts of every member of the community.

This study guide teaches the book. It does not simply use the book as a jumping off point for random conversation. It is written for those persons inside faith communities who continue to look for the practical handles that will make the presence of creativity, justice, and hope more evident in the culture.

This study guide is also written for those outside the faith community as an invitation to see what a faith community can be at its best. One of its goals is to find people to explore faith communities in their own locale in order to challenge them to be involved in this kind of radical engagement.

It is clear in the book that Jacobsen has lived the journey he describes. When I was in the process of introducing him to the Milwaukee community in the late 1980s, his honesty, passion, sense of humor, and track record of organizing in many contexts excited me. Since then, I have taken great pleasure in working with him and observing his gifts in action at Incarnation Lutheran Church, Milwaukee, in our common mission strategy here known as the Milwaukee Lutheran Coalition and through MICAH (Milwaukee Inner-City Congregations Allied for Hope) and the Gamaliel Foundation based in Chicago.

Although not perfect, this congregation-based community organizing stuff works!

Format of the Study Guide

This study guide is organized as twelve adult study sessions that follow the content of the book's chapters. One can simply use less of the discussion material to explore the central theme. The key idea noted in each session can be used for keeping a group focused. The leader may need on occasion to bring the group back to its task. These session plans are designed to keep the conversation guided, yet free for input, discussion, and disagreement.

The objectives of the study guide are threefold:
1) To understand what the author is saying
2) To enter into the situation he is describing
3) To make some claims on how the future may be different.

Jacobsen's work is rich in story, example, and Scripture. In many ways the book teaches itself. The study guide takes advantage of this gift by including discussion of the Scripture and his key stories as ways to enter into the author's discussion and to remind us of similar concerns in our own lives. As participants engage in discussion of the book's key ideas, they will have the opportunity to compare their own ideas with another perspective or worldview.

I recommend that the leader assist the group in being clear what the "either/or" is about in each chapter. What a person decides is his or her own decision. The responsibility of educators is to clarify the options. While presenting the author's view as the argument for congregation-based organizing, the leader is free to guide the discussion to other related issues depending on the interests of the participants.

Enough material is provided here for each session to last two hours. I suggest, however, that each session be limited to seventy-five minutes, starting and ending on time. I further recommend that the leader move through his or her lesson plan (adapted from this study guide) in a disciplined fashion. Even though it is not necessary for all teaching contexts, the timing and punctuality underscore some of the principles of congregation-based organizing. Here is a suggested schedule for each session: *Opening*—15 minutes including the Scripture; *Part I*—20 minutes; *Part II*—30 minutes; *Part III*—8 minutes; *Sendout*—2 minutes.

Session One: The World as It Is

TEACHING OBJECTIVE: To see which realities of life block the future.
LEARNING AIM: To invite the participants to choose between accepting the world as it is and claiming the promise of the world as it should be.

Introduction

1. Personal introductions: Have all participants, one at a time, share their name, the name of their community, and an example of how they have participated in community organizing.

2. Write "Doing Justice" on newsprint, and make a list of images that this phrase suggests to the participants.

3. Read the Scripture from the book's introduction (Hab. 2:1-2).

4. Have each participant write down one vision, purpose, or goal he or she has in choosing to participate in this study.

SCRIPTURE READING: Read the two Scripture readings at the beginning of chapter 1 (John 7:6-7 and Rev. 18:1-4). Take only a few moments (one reading at a time) to get responses to these questions: What prompted the author to include these Scriptures at the beginning of the chapter? What is he trying to communicate to the reader?

I. Understanding the Author's Point of View

Have the participants look at the twelve chapters. Ask them to suggest chapters that could be grouped together. Show on newsprint the following grouping of chapters to provide an overview of the book:

Chapters 1–4: Laying the Groundwork for Congregation-Based Community Organizing (CBO)—situation and possibility

Chapters 5–8: The Foundational Principles of CBO

Chapters 9–12: Next Steps: Implementing the Principles of CBO

KEY POINT: "The world, as it is, is the enemy of God." Read aloud the first paragraph and make a list of how the "world as it is" is described: "driven by abusive power, consuming greed, relentless violence, and narcissistic pride; employs nationalism, propaganda, racism, civil religion, and class enmity to bolster entrenched systems, corporations, and institutions."

a. Discuss this description by having participants give examples from the world and their own lives. This list is heavy. Acknowledge this heaviness, but don't move too quickly to fix-it solutions or sentiments of "things aren't that bad." The point is to try to understand the nature of the situation from the author's point of view.

b. What does the author mean when he says: "All of this is offensive to God and to the people of God"?

c. Discuss the "nightmare" of the author. How do we feel in the midst of these kinds of negative realities? Have you had similar feelings, such as "shutting down emotionally"?

II. Living into This Experience

a. Parcel out the five stories to different people or teams (ten-year-old, Billy, Teresa, Gary, Deborah).

b. Have each team spend a few minutes with the story assigned to them. When the group reconvenes, discuss each story from the point of view of the person in the story. For example: How does Billy see the world?

c. List on newsprint the ways the participants experience religion "being co-opted by the world." (Mention the biblical phrase "coming out of Babylon." What does that refer to?)

d. How is your church denomination or congregation tempted to be co-opted by the world? How is it "coming out of Babylon"?

e. Discuss how people can be personally "charitable, forgiving, and exemplary in their love" even as people of faith, yet in their public life they are constrained to adopt a different ethic.

f. *Quid pro quo* means "exchanging this for that" or making a deal. How does making deals compromise justice in your experience in your community?

III. Making Claims on the Future

a. Have each person take two minutes to draw a geographical outline (boundaries) of their community or neighborhood.

b. In your own community, where are the tensions with the world as it is?

c. Which of these tensions would you like to begin working to change?

Sendout: Go around the room and ask for one word or a short phrase describing today's session. Thank everyone for staying with this discussion about difficult things. In conclusion, ask participants to be prepared next time to talk about "the world as it should be." Read aloud the last two paragraphs of chapter 1 to conclude the session.

Session Two: The World as It Should Be

TEACHING OBJECTIVE: To experience the possibilities of shaping the future. LEARNING AIM: To invite participants to embrace concrete hope over forces that are committed to holding onto power for the purpose of oppressing others.

Introduction

1. Personal introductions: Have all participants, one at a time, share their name and one way they observed the world as the enemy of God this past week.

2. Have the group brainstorm a list (write it on newsprint) of people who in their experience have stood against the forces of evil.

SCRIPTURE READING: Read the two Scripture readings from the beginning of chapter 2 (Matt. 5:2-10 and John 18:37-38). Take a few moments to discuss the author's purpose in using these passages. Ask the participants to relate Pilate's question, "What is truth?" to the teachings of Jesus.

I. Understanding the Author's Point of View

Refer to the three-section breakdown mentioned in session one, indicating that we are at the second part of the initial phase, "laying the groundwork for congregation-based organizing."

Take the list from session one describing "the world as it is" as the left column, and create a right-hand column, with the participants listing the characteristics of "the world as it should be" from the first two paragraphs of chapter 2: "rooted in truth, love, and community . . . the voice of conscience is heard . . . people act according to the values of their faith . . . fairness and mutuality reign . . . God's dream engaging the nightmare that the world has become." And, "persona (mask) is removed . . . trust each other . . . transparent . . . exposed . . . live truthfully . . . honestly . . . with integrity . . . as authentic persons."

Ask the participants how they react and/or feel when they are bombarded with a list like the first column and the second column?

KEY POINT: The world as it should be is in direct opposition to the world as it is.

Have the group discuss the example of the lawyer's dilemma painted by the author. How do the participants "long for such a world and suffer because they do not find it"?

II. Living into This Experience

The majority of this chapter is the description of the author's own passion for "the world as it should be."

a. Have the group retell in some detail the experience of Jacobsen as a campus pastor involved in the defense of Martin Sostre.

b. Have the group imagine themselves as the brother or parent of Jacobsen. What would your ideas have been about his involvement? What fears would you have? What encouragement would you have given him? Would you have advised him to continue or to get out of this situation?

c. Many people have a vision for bettering the world. The author lists a few: Philip and Daniel Berrigan, Martin Luther King Jr., Oscar Romero, Dorothy Day. He calls them "seers of the world as it should be." As a group, list on newsprint the content of the vision of these persons. What is it that they saw as a better world? The author calls this way of looking at the world a moral vision. What does he mean by that? What is an immoral vision? How does one tell the difference? Why is moral vision rejected? The author asks, "Which sane person does not see the imperative of a world free of nuclear weapons?" How would you respond to this question? What accounts for the fact that nuclear weapons exist, to some degree are proliferating, and still threaten our existence?

d. Have the group focus on Nora and her dream of heaven. What is the author demonstrating by comparing adults and children?

e. Discuss the difference between "childlike in its innocence" (the world as it should be) and "pseudo-innocence" ("the affliction of many Christians"). Ask for examples of each from the participants' experience.

f. Discuss the phrase attributed to Martin Luther King Jr. via Paul Tillich: "power without love is tyranny; love without power is sentimentality." Give examples.

III. Making Claims on the Future

a. Who in your community could be allies claiming "the world as it should be"? Give everyone three minutes to make a list. Share.

b. Look at your community map from the first session and fill it in with signs of hope—things going on in the community that combat the powers that manipulate and control. How could you be involved in supporting these groups or making these signs of hope more evident?

Sendout: Go around the room and ask everyone for one word or a short phrase describing today's session. Ask everyone to be aware of the public arena around them as they read next week's chapter. Conclude by using the quote: "'Everyone who belongs to the truth listens to my voice.' Pilate asked him, 'What is truth?'"

Session Three: Engaging the Public Arena

TEACHING OBJECTIVE: The public arena is a challenge and source of fear for the church and its leaders.

LEARNING AIM: To invite participants to deepen their engagement as the church in the public arena.

Introduction

1. Personal introductions: Have all participants, one at a time, share the name of their community/neighborhood with an example of how they

have experienced the "maddening, chaotic pace" of the public arena this past week.

2. Ask participants to imagine themselves as a person in the community who is not a member of the church. What do they think people on the streets say about the church (if anything)? They should imagine not what they would like the people to think, but how the church is actually viewed in public life versus other public institutions such as school, library, and police.

SCRIPTURE READING: Read aloud the two Scripture passages at the beginning of chapter 3 (Matt. 28:19-20; Luke 4:18-19). Discuss which images of these Scriptures are most compelling in inviting the participants to the public arena. Ask for any other insights the group has regarding why the author chose these Scriptures.

I. Understanding the Author's Point of View

Note: This discussion is focused on the last of the introductory chapters.

a. Have the group tell the story of the author's experience of the sanctuary. As the story is told, divide a sheet of newsprint into two parts: sanctuary and streets. Write the descriptive words under each. These lists will have similarities to the early lists of "the world as it is" and "the world as it should be."

b. After making these lists, ask the participants to share how "the attraction of the sanctuary can become a seduction." What is the experience of the participants of the sanctuary? Is it in any way what the author describes? List the following on the newsprint:

- Sanctuary as false catharsis instead of authentic hope.
- Liturgy as disembodied drama instead of an incarnational vision.
- Sanctuary as a comfortable substitute for harsh realities. (outside walls)

How have our churches become a mystery religion? How does a mystery religion lack the power to have an impact on the world as it is? How serious is this situation for the church?

KEY POINT: Biblically speaking, the preeminent activity of the church is in the public arena, not in the sanctuary.

II. Living into This Experience

a. In making his key point, the author talks abut the evangelism mission ("the Great Commission") of the church: "Evangelistic efforts that claim to flow from the Great Commission but ignore or violate the Sermon on the Mount are not only ignoble but also heretical."

    i. Ask the group what point he is making. Mention his example of Dietrich Bonhoeffer's view of the church and "self-preservation." Discuss in what specific ways the group sees the church preserving itself. What is the end result of self-preservation?

    ii. Ask the group why the author is so adamant about this point. How can he call part of the church heretical?

b. "Who takes the local church into the public arena if not the pastor?" How does the author portray "most clergy"? (They are "unwilling to lead their churches into the public arena.") Is that the experience of your participants? How serious an issue do they think it is? What does the author see as the central problem of clergy (ambivalence, reluctance, or disdain toward the public arena)? Have the group give some examples.

c. Discuss the "accommodation theology" of Franz Bibfeldt.

d. Have the group define *civil religion*. How is it worse than accommodation theology in keeping clergy and their churches in the sanctuary?

    i. Relate the Pentagon example. Have the group give other examples.

    ii. List the issues that churches seduced by civil religion tend to support: "capital punishment, military build-up, . . . policies that are punitive toward the poor, immigrants, and people of color."

e. Discuss how churches have responded in positive but limited ways in the public arena. Discuss the difference between a do-gooder and a "doer of good."

f. How does advocacy go beyond charity? How does advocacy fail? (no organizational base)

g. What are the pluses and minuses of resolutions and church social statements?

III. Making Claims on the Future

Have each person put these methods for responding in the public arena in a column: direct service, advocacy, church resolutions, church social statements, other. Draw three more columns to respond to three questions for each method. Have them rate the methods on a 1–10 scale (10 as highest) for each question:

a. Which method have they tended to see as the responsibility of the church?

b. Which have they tended to use themselves for addressing social needs?

c. What has been their level of satisfaction in using each of these methods?

Sendout: Go around the room and ask for one word or short phrase to describe today's session. Mention that these first three sessions have cleared the way for introducing another method for the church to address the public arena: Congregation-Based Community Organizing (CBO). Close with reading Luke 4:18-19.

Session Four: Congregation-Based Community Organizing

LEARNING OBJECTIVE: To grasp the understanding that undergirds CBO.

TEACHING AIM: To offer CBO as an option or supplement to other forms of engaging the public arena on matters of justice.

Note: This lesson plan will not be as detailed as the previous three. Chapter 4 presents a case study of one congregation-based community organization, MICAH (Milwaukee Inner-City Congregations Allied for Hope). It comes halfway through the study and serves as a concrete way of presenting CBO as a clear option for engaging the community. It also gives a specific backdrop for dealing with what will follow, that is, the foundational principles of organizing. Therefore, we have the opportunity for a type of "action-reflection" learning experience: Here is MICAH; here are the stories that demonstrate its value; now let's learn how to do it.

Introduction

1. Personal introductions: What has happened this week in the community that demonstrates the need for more than charity or advocacy?

2. If you were to begin to organize now, what would be on your list of issues?

SCRIPTURE READING: Have the Scripture (Exod. 18:14, 17-18, 24-25) read out loud. If this passage is all you had of the author's thoughts for this chapter, what would you assume might be the subject and focus of the chapter? Discuss the leadership style described here, particularly its strengths and weaknesses.

I. Understanding the Author's Point of View

a. Ask the participants to list on the board the persons mentioned on page 24 (Alinsky, Chavez, King). Pull from the group the stories of each and how they contributed to building a basic philosophy of organizing local grassroots persons.

b. Write on newsprint "Values and Principles"(King) and "Methodology" (Alinksy), drawing an arrow in between pointing both ways. List underneath the following pairs:

   i. Faithfulness and effectiveness

   ii. Morality and expediency

   iii. Conscience and compromise

   iv. Prophetic and practical

   v. World as it should be and world as it is

Discuss the distinctions and the overlaps between the two parts of each pair. Why are both necessary, or are they? What is needed to keep this tension alive and creative?

c. List the four major organizing groups across the United States.

d. Discuss the steps for developing a local congregation-based community organization.

e. This chapter introduces the phrase faith-based organizing. What is your sense of the meaning of this phrase? Some have speculated that organizers use the church because it is the primary institution left, not because of any particular love for the church or its message. What are your thoughts?

KEY POINT: Congregation-based community organizing is rooted in the local congregation.

II. Living into This Experience

a. Have the group describe CBO as rooted in the congregation (pages 30–34).

b. List the achievements of MICAH. Talk about the banking effort and the drug treatment work.

c. Tell the stories of Incarnation Lutheran Church as examples of the effectiveness of CBO—Stephanie, Tamicka, Annette, and Ricardo.

d. What have been the practical growth points for Incarnation's leaders?

III. Making Claims on the Future

a. Have each person look at his or her own neighborhood or community and congregation and write down two or three ways to initiate or strengthen involvement in CBO.

b. Have each person list the obstacles to initiating a new organization, joining a present one, or strengthening current involvement in one.

c. Have each person claim one action she or he will commit to do this week to make CBO a greater reality in the community.

Sendout: Ask each person to share one word or phrase about today's session. Mention that the next sessions will deal with the essential concepts of organizing from a faith perspective. Conclude with this Scripture: "What you are doing is not good. You will surely wear yourself out, both you and these people with you. For the task is too heavy for you; you cannot do it alone" (Exod. 18:17-18).

Session Five: Power

LEARNING OBJECTIVE: To reexamine notions of power.

TEACHING AIM: To begin to sense one's own power personally and corporately.

Introduction

1. Personal introductions: Have participants give their name in the following manner: My name is Rick, and I am a person of power.
2. After all participants have introduced themselves, go around and do it again, staccato like, one right after the other.
3. Ask the group for reactions: (a) What did they notice? (b) How did it feel as a person? (c) Could you identify a group feeling? (d) What is our normal response to naming or being named "powerful"?

SCRIPTURE READING: Read the two Scripture readings at the beginning of the chapter (Acts 1:8; and 1 Cor. 15:24-27). Pause after each for observations connecting the chapter title, "Power," with the Scripture. Ask: What are these Scriptures suggesting that *power* is?

I. Understanding the Author's Point of View

a. Point out that in the flow of the book, this first session on basic principles of organizing (power) will be followed by others: self-interest, one-on-ones, and agitation. Hand out a chart of these four organizing principles, so participants can see their interrelationship and experience them in that way.
b. Write on newsprint: Power and Powerlessness. Ask the participants to give synonyms for each of these words. After you have several for each word, ask for examples of
   i.   Where the participants see each in the world
   ii. How they have experienced each.
   What do these examples suggest about the reality of power?

c. Next write on the newsprint: Principles of Power (taught by organizers) and the Power of Principles (taught by the faith tradition). Under Principles of Power list power analysis, one-on-one interviews, cutting issues, agitating. Under Power of Principles list inner journey, communal journey.

KEY POINT: To exercise the principles of power without the power of principles leads to tyranny. To live out the power of principles without the principles of power leads to sentimentality. Together the principles of power and the power of principles can lead us to justice.

II. Living into This Experience

Tell the Betty Smith story as a backdrop for this discussion. In the light of this story discuss the key points of the chapter relating the story to the points made.

a. Discuss a community organizer's view of power. How is it defined? (Spanish word *poder*) How did Betty Smith view power?

b. What is the source of organizers' impatience with the "ambiguity that people of faith have with power"? Discuss the phrase "most people seek innocence to avoid the responsibility of power." State that sentence in your own words. What is the responsibility of power? Why do folks avoid it? Describe Betty's action if she sought to remain "innocent."

c. Where do you see good people—sitting on the sidelines, wrapped in virtue, allowing other people's values to dominate? Is Betty Smith a good person? Is the alderperson?

d. Why do organizers talk about two sources of power—organized people and organized money? What reality are they recognizing? What reality are they walking into? What are the choices when functioning in the public arena? How could Betty have strengthened her case? How could she have abused power?

e. Is it inauthentic to point out only the abuses of power? What does it mean to say that power is neutral? Someone has said that "the power is in the center of the table."

f. What is your approach to the inner journey? What specific practices, such as meditation, contemplation, and prayer, do you use?

g. Have the group identify a situation in which they are part of a group trying to make a decision. Someone in the group may be on a church or neighborhood committee. Treat it as a case study to examine the issues of power present. Focus them on something the group did once or now has to decide. What does it mean for each person to function with the power at the center of the table?

III. Making Claims on the Future

As background for this section have each person read the Marianne Williamson quotation, "Our deepest fear is not that we are inadequate. . . ." Have persons in the group state in their own words the essence of this statement.

a. Have each person make a list of the groups or associations he or she is a part of, beginning with the family. Have them rate their participation (their use of power) in the group on a basis of 1 (low participation) and 2 (high participation).

b. Have group members take a few moments to write for themselves a description of themselves on the power continuum. For example, "I tend to be a person who lets others make decisions" or "I tend to make decisions without consulting others."

c. Have group members note in their list of associations where they intend to make a new decision about how they participate.

Sendout: Go around the group and ask everyone for one word or a short phrase to describe today's session. Conclude with reading Acts 1:8.

Session Six: Self-Interest

TEACHING OBJECTIVE: To clarify the understanding of *self-interest* as different from *selfishness* or *selflessness*.

LEARNING AIM: To engage the participant in recognizing how she or he views self and to consider a new method of self-discovery.

If I could teach only one chapter of this book, Chapter 6, "Self-Interest," would be it. In this chapter, one wrestles with and may discover a new or renewed sense of "I" in community—Who am I? What will I do with my life? Does not all else flow from this ongoing questioning of life and my life?

Introduction

1. Personal sharing: Have all participants, one at a time, share one way in which they participate in the "inner journey."

2. Write "self-interest" on the newsprint and ask what comes to mind when they see this word. What are synonyms for *self-interest*?

SCRIPTURE READING: Read each Scripture passage aloud (Exod. 3:10-11; Luke 9:23), pausing after each one to respond to the question "Who is being addressed?" What relationships are described in each? What do these Scriptures suggest the chapter may be about?

I. Understanding the Author's Point of View

Note for the participants that along with power, self-interest is the second basic principle of CBO that we have looked at. The next sessions on "one-on-ones" and agitation conclude the discussion of principles and form the foundation for looking at how organizing can be advanced.

Write the words *authentic self* in the middle of the newsprint. Draw an arrow pointing to the left and write "selfishness." Draw an arrow pointing to the right and write "selflessness." You will use this later in the session.

a. Discuss again the public arena as a place where deals are cut. Use the civil rights movement illustration to identify that groups work out of self-interests. Point out the difference between how the government organizes people (force, violence, money, bribery, and propaganda) and organizers who organize around self-interest.

b. Using the visual, ask the group to list the words that describe "selfishness" (ego-centric, self-obsessed, etc.). Do the same with the words describing "selflessness" (saintly, humble, etc.) Write the words *isolated* under "selfishness" and *victims* and *do-gooders* under "selflessness."

c. Have the group discuss their experience with others and themselves as cut off from community either by selfishness or by selflessness. Write "no mutuality" under each.

d. Under authentic self write the word *self-interest*. Write underneath it "honors self/honors others." Give examples of short- and long-term self-interest. Ask the group if they see the differences.

II. Living into This Experience

a. Review the story of Jesus as the "highest form of self-interest." Discuss the term *self-denial*. Ask for examples of how that phrase has been misused and has created a whole church culture of people without a sense of their true selves.

b. Ask for examples of how the participants have seen misuse of self-denial in their own experience of church.

c. Ask which of the two groups (selfishness or selflessness) is the most tempting for them. Give examples.

d. Define and discuss *nihilism* and what it suggests about the need to recover the authentic self through identifying and organizing around self-interest.

    i. Where is nihilism alive and well today?

    ii. What is understandable about why people choose nihilism? Why is it an inauthentic choice?

e. Moses' experience: Recount the "I Am Who I Am" burning bush story (Exod. 3:1 — 4:17). Ask the group to create the setting, the players in the drama, and the verbal exchange.

    i. How does Moses discover his identity and purpose?

    ii. What does it mean to say: "The discovery of true self and true self-interest can only be done in the context of community"? What does it mean for Moses? For us?

KEY POINT: The discovery of authentic self means also a discovery of God. And this discovery is done in community. It is the meaning of God as a relationship we have to life versus God as a being perched up there somewhere in the universe looking down and either manipulating or abandoning the world.

III. Making Claims on the Future

a. What are the "burning bushes" in your life? In other words, on what occasions in your life have you asked the "Who am I?" question?

b. How is the act of claiming one's authentic self an act of courage? What is your experience of claiming your authentic self?

c. Why is it easier to accept a false self than one's own self?

d. Write down three things that you would like to do to make your life more interesting.

e. Look at your list to see whether these activities are informed more by selfishness, selflessness, or self-interest. Be careful. These evaluations are not always obvious because we tend to assume that doing things for oneself is not as noble as doing things for others, such as working at a soup kitchen. Remind the group of the author's story about his first marriage. What interest was being served? For whom?

f. List three steps that you could take to discover your self-interest and act on it in community. (This task is easy until you add the word *community*.)

Sendout: Ask each participant to share the most difficult thing about this session and the most exciting thing. Conclude by reading the closing paragraph of the chapter that ends with the words "standing and moving on holy ground."

Session Seven: One-on-Ones

TEACHING OBJECTIVE: To understand one-on-ones as the primary tool of organizing.

LEARNING AIM: To begin to experience the gift of relationships.

Introduction

1. Personal sharing: Invite participants to share their reflection on and experience of self-interest this past week.
2. Where did they see selfishness or selflessness in others or themselves?
3. What examples of self-interest did they see?

SCRIPTURE READING: Have the Scripture at the beginning of the chapter (John 1:35-39) read aloud. Follow this reading with a more extended discussion than previous sessions.

1. What words jumped out as you heard this passage read?
2. Describe the particulars of the scene as if you were putting on a play and needed characters, props, and lighting.
3. Identify the feelings present in this exchange among John, the other two disciples, and Jesus. What emotions are present in the story?
4. Identify your feelings as this drama unfolds. Describe your emotions.
5. Give a title to this story.
6. What is the story about?
7. What excites you about the story?
8. What confuses you about the story?
9. What do you imagine took place that day? What did they learn about each other?
10. What other stories does this story remind you of?
11. What experiences does it trigger from your own life?
12. With whom do you have relationships?
13. What are you doing to strengthen them?
14. With whom do you want or need to build relationships?

I. Understanding the Author's Point of View

a. Divide the group into pairs—ask each person to choose someone he or she would like to know better—and ask the pairs to talk with each other for ten minutes. Each person has five minutes to find out about the other person. (At this point they are going "cold turkey." You will discuss the principles of one-on-ones later.)
b. Bring the group back together and debrief: (1) What happened? (2) Why did it happen? (3) What does it mean?

c. Make a chart on newsprint with "One-on-One: Initiating or Building a Relationship" at the top. Underneath make columns listing (1) what it is, (2) what it isn't, (3) getting to know you. Then have the group fill in each category:

   i. What it is: (1) a natural conversation; (2) skilled, artful, intentional, focused.

   ii. What it isn't: (1) a sales pitch; (2) asking another person to do something; (3) an attempt to recruit for your cause.

   iii. Getting to know you: (1) learn another person's self-interest; (2) we come to understand what is important to the person, what motivates him or her, and what is his or her passion.

d. How did your conversation reflect this description of one-on-ones?

e. Where do you need strengthening in the one-on-one process?

II. Living into This Experience

a. Discuss the characteristics of an interviewer and reflect on how one would develop these skills: (1) curiosity, (2) courage, (3) genuine interest in the other person, (4) probing to discover motivational depths, and (5) listening for tragedy, pain, anger, passion, injustice.

b. Have the group divide into subgroups of three people. Again give each pair five minutes to do a one-on-one. Have the third person be an observer and share for two minutes at the end of the five minutes what strengths he or she had observed and areas to work on (using the criteria list in point a). Have each person play each role in the threesome.

c. Reflect on learning with the whole group. What are the values of this process? What are the challenges?

d. Describe how the author characterizes Jesus' conversations. (never casual)

   i. Discuss the difference between the questions "What do you want?" and "What are you searching for?" Follow that with discussion of the question, "Whom are you looking for?" which the resurrected One asked of Mary Magdalene.

   ii. Discuss how, according to the author, a sacred conversation occurs. Note the vulnerability and mutual searching consciousness of the person leading the conversation.

   iii. Share the stories of Jesse and members of the church and how the one-on-one worked as a way of discovery in their lives and the life of the author.

III. Making Claims on the Future

a. Have the group share ways the one-on-one could be used in their church or community.

b. Ask each person to commit to doing at least one "one-on-one" in the next week. It will be a thirty-minute encounter with another person, not the five-minute as used in the exercise. The leader may have to give further instruction on this point. The challenge and gift of the one-on-ones is the thirty-minute conversation that reveals much about the person's self-interest.

Sendout: Go around the room and ask for one word or a phrase to describe each person's experience of this session. Read the last three sentences of the chapter to conclude the session.

Session Eight: Agitation

TEACHING OBJECTIVE: To move to an understanding of agitation as necessary in a creative relationship.

LEARNING AIM: To experience a new sense of one's own power, which flows from clarifying one's vision for life.

Introduction

1. Personal sharing: Go around the room and ask, "Did you do a one-on-one this week?"

2. Have participants who answered "yes" share their experience. Was anything clearly a block in keeping others from doing it?

3. Point to accountability as a way to get things done, build a sense of interdependence and team, and stretch us beyond where we might naturally go.

SCRIPTURE READING: Have John 21:15-17 read aloud. Ask these questions:

1. What did Jesus ask Peter? How did Peter respond? How did Jesus answer?

2. How many times did Jesus ask? How many times did Peter respond the same way? What kind of answer did Jesus give?

3. How did Peter feel after the third question?

4. Why did Peter feel hurt? What internal struggle is he having?

5. Is Peter feeling hurt a bad thing? Is it a good thing?

I. Understanding the Author's Point of View

a. Discuss the word *agitation*.

    i.   What are synonyms for agitation?

    ii. What kinds of things agitate people?

    iii. What agitates you?

    iv. Has the word taken on primarily negative connotations?

    v. What creative function does agitation take in life?

    vi. Where have you seen people "do the right thing" because they were agitated?

    vii. What can agitation do that being nice may not be able to achieve?

b. Tell the story of the author's experience at the Gamaliel Foundation training.

    i.   How did Greg agitate Jacobsen?

    ii. In retrospect what has Jacobsen realized about Greg's action?

        1.   An act of care (love) and belief inviting clarity about life

        2.   A skill that summons forth the best.

KEY POINT: Healthy agitation is an act of love that calls people to act out of their own power, self-interest, and vision.

a. Discuss why such a thing as an "outside agitator" is impossible. (Because "relationship is a prerequisite of agitation.")

b. Ask if the participants have experienced guilt-tripping in the church. How does guilt-tripping work? What is the result of using the guilt-tripping method? Describe the difference in the way Jesus deals with Peter (that is, Jesus is direct and honest and only desires that Peter move out of his fear and remorse).

c. Likewise the man by the pool: Describe that story. Agitation is used by Jesus to release the man's potentiality and to enable him to bear into the future that which he has not accepted as his life. To be free he has to be all those other things he had been, not in denial and illusion.

II. Living into This Experience

a. Ask: What is the vision we have for our lives? How do we pick up our mats and walk into the future with power and purpose?

b. Quote from the chapter: "Agitation is a summoning forth of one's vision for one's life. . . . At its best agitation touches on the matter of vocation" (the purpose of one's life).

    i.   Discuss Mother Teresa's "divine call within a call." What does it have to do with us?

    ii. What is your sense of vocation or call these days?

iii. Who or what is agitating you to think in new ways about the purpose of your life? (Note intrusions, challenges, confrontations, tensions.)

iv. How has the church earned the reputation "you speak the truth but you don't do me a darn bit of good"?

v. What would the church look like if it were a place where this kind of honest "stretching" of our lives could take place?

III. Making Claims on the Future

a. Using the example of Nora and Laureena's birth struggle, write down two times in your life when struggle, tension, and risk accompanied some kind of new birth.

b. Take a moment and write your life's purpose on a slip of paper to go inside a fortune cookie. For example, "Martin Luther King Jr., your life purpose is to be a drummer for freedom."

c. What steps do you need to take to begin or continue the movement toward your purpose? For example, the drummer for freedom organized people around a vision of "black and white together" agitating for justice at lunch counters, in the streets, and in the halls of business and government.

d. What kind of agitation are you going to need to move toward your life purpose? Who is going to provide that agitation for you?

e. Who in your life needs some healthy agitation to get moving in life? How might you be the vehicle for healthy agitation?

We have now completed phase two, the basic building blocks that include power, self-interest, one-on-ones, and agitation, which give body to the overall analysis of the world, the public arena, and the church given in the first phase. The final phase includes metropolitan organizing, building and sustaining an organization, community, and spirituality for the long haul—creating the foundation for change.

Sendout: Have group members share a word or phrase that describes their feeling about this session. End the session by addressing the group with the question: "Do you want to get well?"

Session Nine: Metropolitan Organizing

TEACHING OBJECTIVE: To become familiar with a metropolitan image of community and the need to organize people regionally to build healthier communities across the region.

LEARNING AIM: To become willing to engage in the unsettled debate over whether and how metropolitan organizing can be accomplished.

Introduction

1. Have you been agitated this past week? By whom or with what results?
2. Have you participated in agitating someone? What were the results?
3. What are you learning about healthy agitation as a tool for creating new life?

SCRIPTURE READING: Have Luke 24:49 read aloud.

1. What are the key words in this short verse?
2. What kind of power is referenced here?
3. Why do they have to wait for this power?
4. Where will this power take them? (the Father's promise)

I. Understanding the Author's Point of View

Begin with the story of Gary, Indiana.

a. What was it thirty years ago? What is it now?
b. What is happening to the Gary region?
c. Where else are these changes happening?
d. Describe urban sprawl and its effects.
e. What policy are David Rusk and Myron Orfield arguing for?
    i.   Where do they think regionalization is working?
    ii.   Talk about Indianapolis as an "elastic" city and Milwaukee as "inelastic." What does each of those terms do for a city?
    iii. Identify areas you know as inner-, core-, or heart-of-cities.
    iv. Identify areas you know as second-ring suburbs.
    v.   What do these two have in common in terms of self-interest?
    vi. Identify areas you know as wealthy suburbs. Why do they not have the same self-interest?
    vii. Identify the opposition to regionalization: developers of new subdivisions, construction industries, labor unions, fear of encroachment of the racially and economically different city.
    viii.Do you know of businesses and politicians who are beginning to see the wisdom of regionalization?
f. Describe the hope and promise of metropolitan organizing.
g. What are the internal challenges that existing community organizations face when considering broadening their focus and base of operation?

KEY POINT: Congregation-based organizing needs to draw on Scripture and faith as a means of creating the vision and moral mandate needed to overcome the many obstacles to metropolitan organizing.

II. Living into This Experience

a. Discuss vision for organizing combining Christianity's vision for expansion and congregation-based community organizing's fidelity to the justice dimension.

b. Reflect on the Pentecost event in the church as the vision for expansion.

c. Reflect on Paul's struggle with racism and legalism as fidelity to justice.

d. Discuss the external obstacles of race and class.

e. Discuss the internal obstacles demonstrated in the telling of the story of the twelve spies and the land of Canaan.

f. Rehearse the story.

   i. Identify the players.

   ii. What two self-inflicted problems came from the ten spies? (identifying the Anakites as the Nephilim and seeing themselves as grasshoppers)

   iii. How did Caleb counter these issues, and what were the results?

   iv. How does the author use Caleb as an image for what congregation-based organizing needs? (Calebs, of all ages, are out there in our churches.)

III. Making Claims on the Future

What is the author's stance on this issue? What does he think is required for effective metropolitan organizing? (See reality as it is.)

The author uses the credal phrase "the holy catholic church" as an image for the church functioning as one across the boundaries of geography, race, economics, and so on.

a. What may be the special challenge for Christians in the wealthy suburbs?

b. What kind of sensitivity and understanding does the city church need to bring to this dialogue? How can the issues be enjoined without communicating a sense of superiority or self-righteousness by the city churches?

c. Tell and discuss the Zacchaeus story.

d. How is metropolitan organizing not about class warfare?

e. Define your metropolitan area. Name the areas: city, second ring, suburb. In other areas (small town and rural) the dynamics may be present but not named the same way as in a larger city. Regionalization seems to be having an impact on everyone. Rural conferences are more often regional than local.

   i. Describe the relationships among the people in these areas.

   ii.   What kinds of things may touch regional self-interest?

   iii.   Who would be some of the people to do one-on-ones with to begin the dialogue of regionalization and metropolitan or regional organizing?

   iv.   Next week, bring a newspaper article that illustrates the reality of regionalization and/or the need for metropolitan organizing.

Sendout: Go around the group and ask for a word of hope or word of challenge that participants experience as they talk about metropolitan organizing. Conclude with reading the opening Scripture (Luke 24:49).

Session Ten: Building and Sustaining an Organization

TEACHING OBJECTIVE: To become familiar with the journey involved in building and sustaining a congregation-based community organization.

LEARNING AIM: To begin to process for oneself the willingness to be involved in creating or participating in such an organization in your community.

Introduction

1. Share how you encountered the presence of regionalization or need for metropolitan organizing this last week.
2. Share any newspaper articles that participants have brought.
3. Ask what is the most critical issue today in building a metropolitan organization.

SCRIPTURE READING: Have Ephesians 4:15-16 read aloud.

1. How does the phrase "speaking the truth in love" relate to the principles of organizing?
2. What do the terms *joined, knit, equipped,* and *working properly* suggest to you about the organizing task?

I. Understanding the Author's Point of View

Discuss the Nelson Mandela quotation.

a. Who is Nelson Mandela?

b. What has been his life's work?

c. What are the three parts of Mandela's formula for freedom? (meticulous organization, militant mass action, willingness to suffer and sacrifice) Which of those is the most important? The easiest? The hardest? The weakest link in work you see being done by the church or humanitarian organizations?

d. Discuss the dimension of suffering. Where does suffering fit into the Christian story? Rehearse Dietrich Bonhoeffer's story.

e. Discuss militancy and the issues it raises.

f. Discuss meticulous organization. What specifically must be developed if CBO is going to be effective? (core teams, clergy caucuses, leadership training, organizing money, professional staffing, regional and national linking)

KEY POINT: The biblical truth that pronounces vision and the historical truth that discloses organization must both be present to be part of the transformation of creation.

II. Living into This Experience

ACTIVITY: Divide the group into two, one being the *Eros* group, the other the *Logos* group. Give each group fifteen minutes to prepare a short drama (about three minutes in length) demonstrating its role, identity, and function. One group would proclaim, for example, "We are *Eros*!" and give a demonstration of what that looks like. The group can have a few minutes to scan the related information in the chapter to inform the drama.

Have each group present its drama. After it is completed, ask the other group's members what they thought of this presentation. Strengths? Weaknesses?

Return to the whole group, and ask how the people experienced working with each other. What kind of tension was there? What problems are caused if only *Eros* is emphasized? What problems are caused by totally *Logos* persons? How has the group seen this combination misused? Have you ever seen it as complementary?

Ask the group for any insights that would clarify the nature of these realities and how they are interrelated.

III. Making Claims on the Future

a. Rehearse the story of St. Francis and Pope Innocent III.

b. Point out the *Eros* and *Logos* dynamic illustrated here.

c. Assuming that we tend to lean one way or another as persons and organizations, ask each person to identify which direction he or she leans. What is needed in your life to bring balance?

d. As you consider building an organization or simply improving your own life's options or effectiveness, how is *Logos* present? How is it strengthened? How is *Eros* present? How is it strengthened?

e. Write down one thing you will do this week to temper, if necessary, where you are strongest (*Eros* or *Logos*) and one thing you will do to explore a new dimension of your self (*Eros* or *Logos*).

Sendout: Go around the room and ask for one word or phrase to describe today's session. Conclude by reading together the poem on page 84. Then read the last sentences of the chapter (page 86) to the group.

Session Eleven: Community

TEACHING OBJECTIVE: To recognize the possibility of building a just, caring community.

LEARNING AIM: To become a supporter of the congregation-based organizing effort.

Introduction
1. Where did you see or experience *Logos* this past week?
2. Where did you see or experience *Eros*?
3. Where did you see creativity based on a combination of *Logos* and *Eros*?
4. Did you pay attention this past week to your own *Eros* and *Logos* activity?

SCRIPTURE READING: Read Acts 4:32-37 aloud.
1. Give words or phrases from the text that describe this early Christian community.
2. What of this description is familiar to you in your experience?
3. What of this description is foreign to your experience?
4. How does your experience of the church today compare with this description of community?

I. Understanding the Author's Point of View
Tell the story of the author's experience in Tanzania with community.
a. How did he experience the Tanzanian church as community similar to that described in the book of Acts?
b. What did it teach him?
c. What does he say his skepticism about the church being this kind of community is based on?
d. Describe the author's perception/experience of the U.S. church— bland and banal potluck dinners, pseudo-psychological small groups, introspective and innocuous Bible studies. Ouch! What bone is the author picking? (church reflects culture)

e. The author affirms the emotionally invigorating power of hugs, hand-shakes, and hallelujahs, yet he challenges the community of the church to invite the Word to divide soul and spirit, bone and marrow, exposing our complicities and compromises.

KEY POINT: The community called the Christian church must be measured by the historic marks of what it means to be the church—the holy, catholic, apostolic, and confessional church—that is not a future promise or ideal reality, but is in fact the way the church is now. We must live into it for it to be true.

II. Living into This Experience

Make a chart on newsprint with four columns. Put one mark of the church at the top of each column: holy, catholic, apostolic, and confessional.

Have the group share their understanding of each of these by placing the words they would use to describe each mark on the chart. Once they have put several words under each heading, draw a line across the chart underneath their words.

Discuss how the author uses each mark to invite us into a more in-depth understanding of Christians in community.

Holy—to be set apart for God's purposes

a. List the perversions the word *holy* has led to.

b. How does the author recover *holy* as an authentic term for our use to describe the local church today?

c. Discuss how the author sees CBO breaking out of simply mirroring the culture.

d. Discuss the CBO as prophetic. Who does the author say are the unsung prophets? Are his descriptions true in your experience?

e. Take a moment to consider the description of John Paul Sartre's proposition: "Existence precedes essence." Discuss how we must make claims in our life for them to be our truth. It is not simply a matter of assuming commonly assumed attributes—that is, the church is holy, therefore I or we are holy—but rather through an act of courage one must claim holiness. It takes action to call it forth.

Catholic—the universality of the church

a. List the perversions of universality in the church, that is, homogeneity, separation.

b. How can the local church bear the mark of universality ?

c. How does CBO offer a hopeful sign of moving into fulfilling this mark?

d. What does the author mean by *genuine ecumenism*?

Apostolic—the ones who are sent proclaiming victory in the midst of death

a. Give examples of where death has dominion in our lives.
b. Give examples of local apostolic witness that counters these realities.
c. How does CBO offer a path toward being apostolic?
d. Take a moment here to draw an arrow, an arrow with a wide point and wide body.
e. Discuss the images that describe the apostolic witness of people "on the point . . . on the cutting edge," and "where no one has gone before." Recovery of this stance of the people of God may be the most challenging in our century and the next. Write the words Solitary, Vulnerable, Community, Risk, No Justification, and No Rewards out to the right of the arrow. This evaluation is a reinforcement of Sartre's claiming identity and purpose. The group sees that it has a choice either to sustain the existing structures (behind the point) or to venture out onto the point and be part of the change. God loves neither person more than the other. One chooses to step out and the other does not.

Confessional—stance of being holy, catholic, and apostolic as we as the church are before God. (our ultimate concern)

a. Give examples of where we often make our confession. (commitment to meaning)
b. Give examples of the difficulty of being confessional.
c. What is the saving grace of being confessional? Discuss Bonhoeffer: "The deed alone is our confession of faith before the world."
d. What does the church that takes these marks seriously look like?
e. How do we begin to move in that direction?

III. Making Claims on the Future

a. Have each person spend a few moments reflecting on the four marks of the church and then give a description of his or her own congregation's use of these marks. (How are we holy, etc.)
b. Have each person list four actions her or his congregation could do, one in each category, to begin stretching itself, growing toward representing these marks in its corporate life.
c. The decision to follow Jesus or to be the church is first a solitary decision. After you make that decision you join a "community of solitaries" (Bonhoeffer). What is needed to continue to grow in that stance born of an act of courage? Does the church's understanding of being baptized daily help in this regard?

Sendout: Go around the group and ask each person which of the four marks has had the most impact on him or her as the group discussed them. Conclude the session by reading the following statement from the author: "The truth is that the power of the Holy Spirit to create radical community is real and active."

Session Twelve: A Spirituality for the Long Haul

TEACHING OBJECTIVE: To recognize how one becomes bruised and beaten down when "being the church" and doing congregation-based organizing work.

LEARNING AIM: To begin identifying specific tools that are needed to sustain persons and community on the way.

Introduction

1. Have each person share how he or she noticed the four marks of the church—holy, catholic, apostolic, and confessional—this past week (see discussion in session eleven).
2. What primary loyalties did you notice challenge the four marks?
3. Ask folks to share how they are doing as they enter this last session.
4. Have the group recap the overall structure in the three groupings: Sessions 1–4, 5–8, and 9–12. Ask whether they think this grouping holds. Ask whether they would name either individual sessions or the groupings differently.

SCRIPTURE READING: Have 2 Timothy 4:6-8 read aloud.

1. What images from Paul jump out at you?
2. How would you guess Paul was doing at this point—mentally, physically, and emotionally?
3. What does it mean to "pour out one's life"?
4. What finally gives Paul staying power?

I. Understanding the Author's Point of View

a. Review how the author has asked us to consider "justice as an invitation into an interesting life."
b. What kinds of things does one run into in working for justice?
c. Give examples of mistaking frenetic activity for working for justice.
d. With the culture using terms like *workaholism* and *burnout* to describe those who live their lives as people of action, are those who work for justice around the clock justified in doing whatever is necessary as long as it's needed? What is the danger in living within the illusion of fixing things?

KEY POINT: Amidst such realities (sacrifice, risk, loss), what keeps one going year after year, decade after decade, is the presence of Life itself with all of its *yes*, call, creativity, humanity and a tradition and future that continue to offer the promise of fulfillment.

II. Living into This Experience

a. Gather from the group all of those experiences that drain the human being of spirit.
b. Which of these experiences do you know? Give examples.
c. What do we say to ourselves when the struggle is "too deep for words"?
d. What do we do or to whom do we go hoping for refreshment, inspiration, and energy for the new day and its call to work once more for justice?
e. Discuss the author's insight into "the prophetic yes." (Review Jeremiah's story.) What are the characteristics of the prophetic yes? (life affirming, seeks the source of life, a human enterprise)
f. Discuss the author's use of iconography.
   i.   What is iconography?
   ii. What are its history and purpose?
   iii. The author calls iconography and congregation-based community organizing parallel streams. Draw out the parallels that he makes.
   iv. Discuss especially his parallels between the holy face and the human face. Share his insights into healing and removing the mask.

III. Making Claims on the Future

a. Have each person list three ways that he or she works for justice.
b. Have each person list three ways she or he experiences draining of the Spirit.
c. Have each person write a few sentences on what he or she does for sustenance and renewal.
d. Bring the group together to share the things they do for sustenance.

Sendout: Ask the group what they would name this experience they have had during this time together. Then ask each one to share one thing he or she is going to do in a new way. Thank them all for the gifts they have brought to the group and claim a future for the participants individually and if appropriate as a group. Conclude with a reading of the story of "the old rabbi" in this final chapter.